TEXAS COUNTRY COOKING

AT THE HOUGHTON RANCH

LARRY ROSS

SIMON AND SCHUSTER • NEW YORK

NANNY'S

TEXAS
TABLE

Published by Simon and Schuster
A Division of Simon & Schuster, Inc.
Simon & Schuster Building
Rockefeller Center
1230 Avenue of the Americas
New York, New York 10020
SIMON AND SCHUSTER
and colophon are registered trademarks
of Simon & Schuster, Inc.

Designed by Bonni Leon

Illustrations courtesy of the Dover Pictorial Archive Series
Photographs from the Houghton Ranch family albums
Manufactured in the United States of America
1   3   5   7   9   10   8   6   4   2
Library of Congress Cataloging-in-Publication Data
Ross, Larry, date.
Nanny's Texas table.

Bibliography: p.
Includes index.
1. Cookery, American—Southwestern style.
2. Cookery—Texas.   3. Houghton, Martha, 1894–1983.
I. Title.
TX715.R838   1987   641.59764   87-9518
ISBN: 0-671-62534-9

FOR THE RANCH

CONTENTS

CONTENTS

NANNY'S AMARILLO TOWNHOUSE AT
1700 POLK STREET—DESIGNATED AN
ARCHITECTURAL LANDMARK
FOR ITS CLASSIC ''PRAIRIE'' DESIGN

PREFACE

If Martha Houghton's reputation for West Texas cooking was exceptional, it was certainly enhanced by her recipes, which were cherished by her family and friends. Indeed, her happy table was the result of generous exchanges of foodstuffs, prepared food, and the recipes themselves.

"Nanny" always shared fresh produce, eggs, and dairy products from the Ranch with enthusiastic family and friends. It seems as though her station wagon was always chockful of baskets, buckets, and pails of Ranch-raised foods destined for a friend's or neighbor's kitchen. And, needless to say, the many grateful recipients returned her kindnesses with a wide variety of comestibles that usually featured ingredients from the Ranch. Predictably, these grateful exchanges frequently came with intriguing recipes.

Martha Houghton was just as generous with her own recipes and shared as many as she received. As a result, her legacy lives on. She always said she didn't understand why someone wouldn't divulge the secret of some delightful dish. The recipes presented here were her favorites and those she adapted from family and friends. Not infrequently, they were passed on to others and evolved even further. In this collection, for example, a recipe for creamed corn casserole has become an almost soufflé-like Corn Pudding to be triumphantly served along with freshly caught mountain trout—a long distance from the Ranch where it was typically served with chicken fried steak.

But the recipes presented here are really the favorites that made it to Martha Houghton's table. These same recipes went through many adaptations by the many cooks of varying skills who came to work at the Ranch. By necessity, the recipes had to be simple and straightforward—easily followed by cooks who had little experience or time to prepare them.

There was so much to do in a day at the Ranch. The pace was not unlike the one most of us lead in today's more urban environment. Good food prepared in reasonably short time from easily available ingredients still is an important, everyday objective at a working ranch. Therefore, beyond sharing the wealth of this down-home, Texas cuisine, it is hoped that the simplicity of Martha Houghton's approach makes these recipes equally accessible and easy to follow for your own comfort and pleasure. They certainly succeeded at the Houghton Ranch; I hope they will in your home, too.

ACKNOWLEDGMENTS

There are almost as many people to thank for making this book about Nanny and the Houghton Ranch as there are recipes and anecdotes. The summer after Nanny passed on, I was back at the "Headquarters," as the ranch house itself is known, and Lisa Morton, her granddaughter, paid me the sincere compliment of saying that next to herself, she knew of no one who cared more about the Ranch than I. Needless to say, I was touched, and I vowed to do whatever I could to help carry on the traditions of a place that has become so important to us all. This book is a first step, but it could not have been taken without the aid of lots of family and friends.

Besides Lisa, Nanny's daughter Martha Garner and her other granddaughter Martha Bivins have been terrific. They put up with my comings and goings at odd times, and they made my many trips to the Ranch to research Nanny's records or local history as convenient and comfortable as possible. Their interest and enthusiasm has really been quite rewarding. I am only sorry that Martha Garner is no longer with us to enjoy what we've put together.

Another invaluable family source was my mother, Mrs. H. J. Ross, whose fifty-year bond with Martha Houghton gave her a wealth of information regarding Nanny, her hospitality, and the Ranch. I will always be indebted to Mother because of her special relationship with Nanny. Without it, I might never have enjoyed Nanny's influence and interest or, most important, all those wonderful summers at the Ranch which gave me my own wealth of experience to draw on. The process of writing this book only enhanced my appreciation of this legacy.

I am not alone, though. Many family and friends generously shared their own stories and recipes from Nanny and the Ranch: E. C. "Ted" Houghton (Unc's nephew), Jack Shelton, Bill Craddock, Yan Ross, H. J. "Doc" Ross, J. T. Mann, Velma Craig, Alva T. Franklin, Lillie and Gar Osgood, Eva Robinson, Earl Moon, Bessie Hanbury, and Ronnie Hanbury. Carole Lalli, my editor, opened my eyes and ears regarding what to look and ask for. Attorneys Randy Morton and Felix Kent kept the peace; John Burn's hardware and software processed the data—with Donald Bahr's kind help.

Then there's a very special crew who never knew Nanny or the Ranch, but worked tirelessly to get this book into print. Early on, Martha Reddington, Manager of Simon & Schuster's Special Markets, recognized my vision of a book about Nanny and the Ranch. Her friendship and encouragement have been uniquely catalytic and even inspiring. Sometimes when the going got a bit tough, I'd muse over the fact that her first name is Martha, that she had a dear Nanny too, and I'd wonder if Nanny hadn't sent me an angel after all.

Next up for sainthood are two patient ladies, Hope Farrell, who professionally tested Nanny's recipes, and Denise Locust, who typed every word that it took to produce this manuscript—75,000 in all. I extend my thanks to Hope's husband Jim, and their children Pammy and Jamie ("The Little Gourmet") and to Denise's family as well, for their goodwill and support during the many days of hard work Hope and Denise spent making this book as good as it is.

INTRODUCTION

Texas. If cattle and oil wells are its state of mind, then surely "country" is the state of its table. It's here that South and East met West as hearty pioneers added the fiery flair of Mexican cooking to help cope with the heat and harshness of this incredibly big land. Southern planters, slaves, New Englanders, Scots, Germans, and many, many Spaniards who settled in this state produced a school of cooking that's as big in flavor as Texas itself. Its solid, square fare often packs a wallop and not infrequently engenders a good time as well. Call it happy food, comfort food—just mention chicken fried steak or apricot cobbler, barbecue or chili and see if someone's eyes don't light up!

Indeed, a taste for Texas country cooking is like a brand on a steer. Once acquired, it's there for life. I got mine early on as I lived out the boyhood fantasy of spending summers on a real working cattle ranch. For a kid from the East, the experience was bigger than the Lone Star state. Exciting. Enthralling. My fondest childhood memories are tied to this ranch—the Houghton Ranch—and the terrific cooking of its grand, old matriarch, Martha Houghton. To my generation, she was "Nanny."

Just ask anyone who knew her and they will inevitably mention Martha Houghton's cooking and hospitality. They will always have a fond recollection of a dish, a meal, or party they enjoyed at her cattle ranch or Amarillo townhouse. For sure, good food and the Houghton Ranch were always connected to this truly grande dame of the Texas Panhandle.

The only daughter of a wealthy rancher, John Shelton, Martha Houghton was born in 1894 and learned the importance of good, hearty food early on. Shelton was a leading cattleman bent on building one of the great ranches of Texas and in the cattle business became a king among barons. He began each day at 4:00 A.M. with fried chicken or steak before leaving for long day on the range, where he eventually amassed extensive holdings that spread into ten counties and over 248,000 acres. When Martha was only twelve, her mother abandoned the dusty streets of Amarillo for the greater sophistication of Oklahoma City and Martha was left to care for her two young brothers and hard-driving father. Finding someone else to get up in the middle of the

MARTHA HOUGHTON, AGED 18, 1912

JOHN M. SHELTON, CATTLEMAN, ABOUT 1895

night to prepare the great dinners Shelton expected was impossible in this uncouth cattle country, so young Martha took on the chore. It turned out to be one she relished—the matter of providing good wholesome food to stoke the engines of family, friends, and help became her lifelong preoccupation.

No one ever got up from Martha Houghton's table hungry and she saw some pretty big eaters come and go in her day. Her husband, Ted Houghton, was a big man with a big appetite and an even bigger sense of humor. They both loved company, so the Ranch was always full of family, friends, and gales of laughter. Uncle Ted—"Unc" for short —loved a good story, and the atmosphere at dinner could get just as spicy as Nanny's cooking.

Seeing everyone so enthusiastic and filled with pleasure was very important to Martha Houghton. Needless to say, with Dalhart being the closest town some forty miles away—and Amarillo nearly ninety—anyone at the Ranch at mealtimes was asked to stay. I often wondered, though, if some of her guests didn't time their visits to be included in these incredible dinners! Still, no matter how many helpings were offered or requested—seconds, thirds, or more—she always wanted to know, "Did you get enough to eat?"

Oh, how we ate! Lunch—dinner as they say in that part of the country—is the big meal of the day. At the Houghton Ranch, it was a veritable feast. Almost everything served was raised right there and anything that was in season made it to the table in scores—four or five vegetables, an entrée, salad,

MARTHA
HOUGHTON
AND HER
TWO
BROTHERS
MALCOLM
(*LEFT*) AND
JIM, 1902

freshly baked bread, rolls, or biscuits, a host of condiments, and dessert.

If I had to recall a particular meal, it would be Nanny's fried chicken—small, tender, crispy; fried pieces, generously spiked with salt, pepper, and paprika. Breast pieces were quartered rather than halved for quicker cooking and a lighter taste. The crust was a wonderful butterscotch color, the meat rich and moist with the chickeny flavor of well-fed fowl. Cream gravy, a West Texas staple, added a luxurious touch to the chicken and coarsely mashed potatoes. Black-eyed peas, summer squash mashed with onion and hard-cooked eggs, okra, green beans with ham hocks, or corn on the cob were just a few of the vegetables that might have been part of the day's fare.

A salad would round out the vegetables, frequently a large platter of thickly sliced beefsteak tomatoes with thin slices of sweet, translucent Spanish onions—or better yet, wilted lettuce. Butter crunch leaf lettuce fresh from the garden was tossed with bits of bacon, scallions, and a hot, pungent vinaigrette made with bacon drippings and a sprinkle of sugar in place of the oil.

Hot biscuits, rolls, or corn bread with freshly churned butter and homemade preserves were always in ample supply. Jelly made from plums that grew wild on the banks of the arroyo, five miles away in the "far pasture," is something I remember well. So tart, these little plums needed nothing but sugar to make bright red jelly. Three bean salad, deviled carrots (marinated, really), and homemade pickles or watermelon rind added sweet, piquant counterpoints to food that was often spicy or hot.

Then, of course, came dessert. With so many good ones, it's hard to choose which to mention first. Toasted pound cake made with a half-dozen eggs and 7-Up would be a good place to start. Served alongside freshly cranked Peach Ice Cream, it was pure ambrosia. Hot Apricot Cobbler with cream so thick it was lumpy deserves equal billing—but there's no need to stop there. Chess Pie, Lemon Meringue Pie, Pineapple Sherbet, Devil's Food Cake, and Sweet Potato Pudding were just as popular. In fact, Nanny was so loved for desserts and sweets, her recipes in this category outnumbered all others almost two to one!

So, if everyone knew Martha Houghton for her cooking, she knew them as well for their favorite dish or recipe. Everyone had one and it was a delicious point of recognition to be told that something being served had been made with you in mind. Wilted Lettuce Salad for my father, Eggplant Fritters for Nanny's granddaughter Lisa, Ranch Fried Steak for longtime family friend J. T. Mann. The list went on and on. I remember how good I felt as a child when I was told that something I really liked was made just for me.

Even years later, long after college, when I'd return for my annual visit, I'd feel a special welcome when Nanny had Scalloped Tomatoes served at my first dinner "home." If some people have a knack for names and dates, Nanny had one for people and food. Serving your favorite dish was her way of letting you know she was glad to have you at the Houghton Ranch.

Another example of Martha Houghton's thoughtful hospitality relates to just plain water. Right inside the front door at her house in town was a little table with a Victorian pitcher and two silver goblets set on a tray, ready to quench any visitor's thirst in the blistering Texas heat. I can see that silver service now. Beads of sweat would glisten on the pitcher and the shining goblets became frosty when ice water was poured into them. Even when Martha Houghton gave her home to the Junior League for use as its clubhouse and moved to an apartment, the tray with its pitcher and goblets went with her as her continuing symbol of hospitality.

The drink at the door is a clue to Martha Houghton's interest in cooking to please and even surprise. Her southern origins strongly influenced her choice of vegetables and dessert, but entrées and seasoning definitely turned to the Texan penchant for barbecue and Mexican ingredients. She knew the tastes of spices indigenous to her environment and she excelled at bringing them together. If her cooking was not unique, certainly her approach was.

South often met West when she served chili-flecked sausage with eggs and grits or summer squash mashed with onion, hard-cooked eggs, and a healthy dose of pepper. Or Nanny might serve a delicate corn soufflé flavored with jalapeños. This is another example of a vegetable associated with southern tables but enlightened by another influence, in this case, by a little Mexican fire.

Then, there's the matter of barbecue. The taste of meat slow-grilled over mesquite and basted with a hot, pungent sauce is legendary in cattle country. Which cut of meat to use, which wood, and what to serve with barbecue are popular controversies. Martha Houghton often satisfied her guests' hankering for barbecue with a hot, smoked tenderloin sliced paper paper thin and served on biscuits with sweet onions and horseradish as well as barbecue sauce. For more earthy fare, she served pinto beans with short ribs or brisket in the tradition of the chuck wagon and offered stewed apricots for dessert.

As I said, most everything that was served was raised right at the Ranch. The quality was as impressive as the quantity. Fruits and vegetables were picked at their peak of perfection. Corn was harvested just as the kernels became full, long before they turned to starch. Summer squash was never allowed to grow more than six inches long. Meat and fowl were raised to be prime and tender. Beef and pork were carefully "finished" with corn and grain, then hung after slaughter to age in the huge "walk-in" refrigerated room until they were knackered as needed. Chickens were raised with equal care in pens so large they might as well have gone "free range." The result was a bird that was plump and robust with flavor. The eggs were unlike anything available in supermarkets today, not mass produced white eggs in delicate shells with pale yellow yolks and watery whites. These were brown. The shells were so hard they required an extra rap to crack them open and allow the rich, orange yolk and thick whites to ooze into a sizzling pan or a mixing bowl. Even the milk was served in its natural state—unpasteurized and unhomogenized—with little globules of yellow-orange butterfat floating on top—straight from the cows.

What was so special beyond the freshness and abundance of all this food, though, was the Ranch itself, which was so much a part of Martha Houghton's persona. So, even though this book is about Martha Houghton's cooking, it would be impossible to separate her approach to cooking from the Ranch she loved so well.

The Houghton Ranch was, and still is, both a working cattle ranch and a truck farm. Located in the cattle country northwest of Amarillo, it is forty some miles from the nearest town and enjoys a bucolic setting. The terrain is at once rough and rolling—not at all flat as all of Texas is thought to be—and is alluring in its breathtaking openness. It's big country, tens of thousands of acres, with views for miles and miles wherever you turn. The earth is so great and the sky so vast, it's as though the earth hugs the sky. Here and there, cattle graze in pastures that stretch out like tweed carpets, which change in hue with the season. A bland gray in winter, the range turns a silvery green in spring, then gives way to a flaxen gold in late summer and fall. To add to the contrast, ragged red ribbons of clay buttes and white "calèche," or limestone, washouts deck the Ranch with parched earth tones that cause the land to seem to dissolve into the sky at the horizon. The land looks as through it could float on and on forever.

At the center of this ponderosa is an oasis of several hundred acres—isolated and very rare for the High Plains. The waters of three spring-fed lakes nurture acres and acres of orchards, truck gardens, and century-old cottonwoods that shelter the old adobe ranch house from the harsh West Texas sun.

From the main road two miles away, the oasis looks like a great, green meandering wagon train traversing its way across the sandy range. Close up, though, a network of orchards and gardens line up like chevrons along the creek that flows down the middle of this Panhandle Eden. Tomatoes, peppers, eggplant, okra, corn, and beans grow row after row. Squash, melon, and cucumbers planted in hills are cultivated in seemingly endless variety. Lettuce, beets, greens, and potatoes hold their own as well. The orchards are just as prolific. Trees bearing peaches, plums, apples, pears, apricots, and cherries stand in long, arched corridors. The sun filters down through their leaves like shafts of light into a cathedral. Even after tractors had completely replaced horses and mules, a jenny was kept to help in the fields. William, the gardener, loved to cultivate with the help and company of a mule. For years, he could be seen treading behind Ruby, guiding a light plow between the rows of corn and beans.

The center of activity, though, is the ranch house. Affectionately called "Headquarters," part of this old adobe manse was built by Spanish sheepherders in 1840. Later, it served as a stagecoach stop and today, the atmosphere is as rich as the food. A wonderful blend of period furniture and art within the two-and-one-half-foot thick walls reflects a long, charming history. Rough plastered walls are painted a warm cream and the trim a festive blue. Authentic colonial and English pieces that made their way west in a covered wagon, and the high Victorian style that arrived with a fortune made in cattle, mingle well with the burnished pine of a style known in the Southwest as "territorial." Oriental rugs and Navajo blankets and a great collection of family portraits, memorabilia, and Southwestern art give the Headquarters a homey look and touch.

Headquarters was but a stage for Martha Houghton's hospitality and style. The ambience was always cheerful, bright, and ample. Tables set with blue Mexican hand-blown glass and the famous Blue Danube "Onion" pattern looked smart on primitive straw mats. Serving pieces were as eclectic as Nanny's travels and friends. A favorite dish frequently used to serve mashed summer squash was a calico-blue Copeland Spode pattern called "Straw Flowers." Even with a chip in its wide border, the bright yellow squash always looked appealing when presented in this old-fashioned piece.

Flowers were also very much a part of this scenario. Garden-grown flowers were arranged throughout the house, but they were especially stunning in the dining rooms. Huge bouquets that opened out like so many rays of the sun were favorites. Vessels or vases, like Nanny's serving pieces, set off their contents; never quite plain, and not necessarily perfect, they were surely interesting—an unpolished copper pitcher, a miniature barrel with bright brass hoops, an old, square Delco-Remy dry-cell jar, or Victorian ironstone.

Cutting flowers for the Headquarters was first on Martha Houghton's long list of daily chores to be done at the Ranch. She was up at dawn every morning to maintain the many arrangements throughout the house of Spanish zinnias, snapdragons, peonies, and roses all in bright shades of yellow, red, and orange. I can see her now, Nanny's familiar figure, then in her late seventies, moving slowly across the great lawn that stretches from the house to the rose garden where she'd make her cuttings for the day. The mourning doves would still be cooing over the arrival of dawn and she'd be there snipping, snipping in her consistent, deliberate way. She always wore a faded, blue smock and old-fashioned "sensible" tie-shoes with chunk heels; her silver-gray hair would be pulled back and pushed up with a black velvet bow in the style of the Gibson girl she was at the turn of the century. This was one old lady who even in her fragile, later years was lovely, elegant, and still all business. She knew what she wanted, too—so much so, that Neiman-Marcus, her favorite place to shop, would open its Dallas store for her on Sundays.

Nanny was not without a sense of humor, though, and it was as arid as the High Plains. Just before she died, she hired a gardener from Amarillo who proved to be unfamiliar with ranch life. Not long after he arrived, he came running breathlessly into the house, saying, "Miz Houghton, Miz Houghton, they's a rattler in the garden." Stiff with arthritis, Nanny slowly made her way out to the garden where she looked down on a rattlesnake barely twelve inches long. "Quick," she snapped. "Get me a flyswatter; I'll kill it!"

The garden, though, was but one element of her very full routine. She respected efficiency and it served her well. Martha Houghton was a highly organized individual. Even the way she stacked pots in her kitchen for easy access reflected her straightforward approach to her recipes. There wasn't time to hunt for anything. Running the Ranch and pursuing a very active social life made for a very busy day.

Dairy chores were another early morning activity. Every morning, milk fresh from the cows had to be strained and separated. It may sound simple, but cleaning a centrifugal separator makes cleaning a Cuisinart seem like child's play. Nanny loved to churn her own butter and pat it into perfect, half-pound pills, about four inches in diameter and one inch high. And on each she ever made, there were three little hash marks like so many stripes of approval.

Some kind of food was always being prepared or processed. Canning, freezing, putting up preserves, and preparation for proper storage required much time and attention. Meat that was needed for the day's meals had to be cut from carcasses of Ranch-raised beef or pork that hung in the huge walk-in refrigerator. Nanny would have a side or quarter taken out by someone stronger and placed on a great stump that served as a butcher block; then, she would have him cut what she thought was needed. At times, processing took on grand proportions. One recipe for pork sausage indicated quantities of spices to produce one hundred pounds! At least once or twice a week there was ice cream or sherbet to be made, cranked by hand. Of course, it was a pleasant chore; our reward was licking the paddles when the ice cream was ready.

After her husband's death in 1957, Martha Houghton became involved in running every aspect of the Ranch. Even if she could not do the work herself, she was well-versed on the subject and had very definite ideas on how it should be done. Whether it was gardening, building fences, doing structural maintenance, or tending livestock, she knew what had to be accomplished.

In the garden, onions were to have the dirt hoed high around their stems and also be well-irrigated. This labor-intensive method produced onions as sweet and mild as any that ever grew in Vidalia, Georgia. Later they would be plaited and hung in an old adobe hut to cure for winter use. Melons had to be planted just east of the apple orchard in full sun. Tomatoes were picked just before their peak of ripeness and placed in screen-covered boxes in the shade to achieve their final perfection. As for eggplant, it was left to ripen until it was just about to be burned by the scorching Texas sun. Okra, squash, and zucchini were all picked young and tender. Whatever had to be cultivated, watered, or picked, Nanny knew just when and how.

Watering was another major daily chore, without which there would have been no farm or garden. Pumping water from the creek was a delicate operation. If it was not done properly, there would be either no pressure or too much—with pipes bursting and floods sure to follow.

The business of cattle ranching went on, as it still does, almost 'round the clock. The Headquarters area was run like a self-sufficient farm; outside the oasis huge herds of cattle grazed in pastures that stretched as far as the eye could see. Long before daybreak cowboys would saddle their horses in the dark, load them into trailers hitched to pickup trucks, and take off to do the chores required of a man and his mount. Miles away, in pastures of thousands of acres, there would be cattle to herd from one place to another, animals to check for disease and, if necessary, lasso and doctor on the spot. Mending fence, setting out salt or feed, and maintaining stock tanks could take hours of lonely work.

When Nanny and Unc took over the Ranch from her father in 1915, cowboys still traveled everywhere on horseback. They'd leave the Headquarters long before sunup and would frequently be gone until well after sundown, even camping out if they had to. Feeding cattle was done with a wagon and team; hay was made with horse-drawn machinery and many, many hands. Later, pickup trucks and trailers made shorter work of ranching. Cattle were fed from trucks and hay making became so mechanized, it could be done by a few people where it once took a dozen. One thing remained the same, though: Cattle were always "worked" with a horse.

If there wasn't work to be done in the pastures, there was almost always something going on at the shipping pens. A great maze of paddocks and working chutes, the pens were constructed of silver-painted welded pipe built six feet high to serve a variety of functions. A labyrinth of chutes allowed hands to work on cattle hundreds at a time. They could be weighed, branded, polled (dehorned), or treated for sickness almost simultaneously. Cattle arriving at the Ranch for the first time were held at the pens for observation before releasing into the rest of the herd. Cattle on their way to feedlots or market were rounded up and held here until the double-decker tractor trailers came to take them away.

Before trucking, cattle were herded many miles to pens alongside the Rock Island Railroad in Romero.

There, they were loaded twenty-six to a car and shipped out thousands at a time. In those days, "roundup" took far longer. And a chuck wagon was dispatched to feed the hands during the drive, which could take several days. Lots of friends came out to the Ranch to help, and from the looks of the home movies that Nanny made in the early thirties, roundup

and branding clearly became fun social occasions as well. Dinner, of course, was the reward—whether it was at the chuck wagon or in the dining room at the Headquarters.

Whether it was cattle ranching or farming, somehow Nanny kept track of everything. At the same time, she maintained a very active social life and served as a very attentive parent figure. There was always a steady stream of visitors to the Ranch. The two-bedroom guesthouse and assorted spare bedrooms in the ranch house enjoyed a better occupancy rate than the best hotels. Then there were the shopping trips to New York and junkets abroad. Some of those trips must have included some fine dining, for Nanny's cooking occasionally included recipes with origins far from the Texas Panhandle. Twice a year, she made the trip to New York to see the Broadway shows and the latest in fashions with my mother. I remember that when the Twist was "in" (and she was in her early seventies) Nanny just had to go to the Peppermint Lounge to try the new step. Of course, there was plenty to do in Amarillo. She was involved in local events and causes, and played cards every Wednesday without fail with her lady friends. She

ROMERO SHIPPING PENS, NOVEMBER 1934. LOADING CATTLE ONTO THE ROCK ISLAND RAILROAD, 26 HEAD TO A CAR.

no more wanted to miss her poker game than the best Broadway show!

Nanny was terrific at whatever she did and she did it well into her eighties. She was also fast. At the age of seventy-six, she got stopped for driving 90 mph within the town limits of Amarillo! Even now, all of us children —grandchildren, nieces, nephews, and those of us children of close friends lucky enough to call the Ranch "home" for the summer, marvel at Nanny's ability to get things done. Of course, we chuckle, too, over her equally acute ability to press us into service with directives like, "while you're sittin' there doin' nothin' . . ."

These recollections have little to do with food directly, but everything to do with Martha Houghton's strict, disciplined ways. Indeed, her style definitely influenced her approach to cooking the recipes her family and friends remember best. In researching her recipes for this book, one in particular stands out: The recipe was for sour cream cake and was found scribbled on the back of an envelope. The ingredients were listed, the method of mixing noted, and the recipe then concluded with another straightforward directive from Nanny herself, "Now go on and make your cake."

No nonsense; that was Nanny. Before we left for her funeral in October 1983, those of us who had been asked to be pallbearers were admonished by her granddaughter Lisa, "Now remember, stand up straight. Nanny'll be back to get you if you don't!" We laughed. Lisa was right. Nanny never missed a thing. We didn't get away with much, but we loved her. She expected a lot of herself and those around her. Compliments were spare, but genuine. Her pursed lips would break into a gentle grin and you'd know she was amused or pleased. It could be the simplest thing—like a job well done. Nanny was tough but an altogether charming, loving woman.

Understandably, Martha Houghton's need for simplicity was critical. Her lifestyle called for good food that was reasonably quick and easy to prepare. Because she had little time or patience for errors, recipes had to be uncomplicated and easily followed. Nanny's role in the kitchen was supervisory; she did not have time to cook much herself, and cooks with varying degrees of skill had to follow her directions. Good help was hard to find . . . and harder to keep. The turnover in the kitchen was high. They would come out to the Ranch but would remain just a few days or weeks. Most would not stay so long so far from family. Others could not adhere to her regimen. "Norma Jean [or whoever it was that week or month], you don't have your pots stacked right," was a familiar reprimand.

That is not to say, though, that Nanny did not enjoy the dedicated help of several wonderful people throughout the years. Alva T., her cook in town, was with her from 1947. William, her gardener, and Rube, the foreman, farmed the fields and took care of the Headquarters for many, many years. Later, Lillie and Gar Osgood came to the Ranch and cared for the place as if it were their own. To this day, Lillie continues to keep the house decked with bouquets in Nanny's style and the larder filled with our favorite edibles. Gar keeps things running like a well-oiled clock.

So, Nanny's style was taught to many. Her need to teach new cooks or aspirants made her terrific at simple, direct instruction. This is not to say, though, that everything always went smoothly. In one instance, Nanny went away for the day and left instructions to bake a cherry pie. On her return, she found it had been made perfectly—with maraschino cherries!

Today, the Houghton Ranch continues on. Great numbers of cattle still roam its vast pastures and the oasis is farmed much as it was in Nanny's day. Ruby, the mule, the cows, pigs, and chickens are gone, but the horses remain both for working cattle and for her great-grandchildren's pleasure. As for her Amarillo townhouse, it has been designated a historic landmark and is called "Houghton House" by the Junior League, who use it as their clubhouse.

A FAVORITE PHOTO OF

NANNY, AGED 75

The traditions of Martha Houghton are very much alive and well. Her granddaughters Lisa Morton and Martha Bivins carry on with much enthusiasm. And thanks to the dedicated help of Lillie and Gar, the Houghton Ranch is just the way Nanny left it. So much so, that when I return for my annual summer visit, I never fail to enjoy Nanny's Scalloped Tomatoes or sense Nanny's presence among the cottonwood as she makes her way to the garden to cut the flowers she loved so well.

MARTHA HOUGHTON, COWGIRL, 1915

SOUPS

Extremes in weather and temperature are a part of life at the Ranch. Blistering heat is counterbalanced by winter freezes that often dip well below zero for days on end. Indeed, the High Plains is known as the coldest place in Texas. Folks in these parts like to joke that the only thing between them and the North Pole is a barbed wire fence!

Hot winds, northers, blizzards, and hailstorms tear across the Plains constantly. The wind rarely, if ever, lets up. These are good times for soup, cold soup to cool off and hot soup to thaw out. Martha Houghton had enough recipes for either condition.

Among the hot soups, corn chowder is my favorite. This hearty corn-flavored broth is fortified with tasty bits of bacon, potatoes, and onions; ground chile and pepper are spicy reminders that in Texas, for every cold day there are at least two that are hot.

Cold soups were particularly appealing to Nanny— maybe to help cope with the greater number of scorchers. Or, they might have been just another way to indulge in her fondness for fresh vegetables. The potatoes, cucumbers, and tomatoes and peppers pop with flavor in her satiny, cold versions of vichyssoise, cucumber soup and gazpacho. Hot or cold, though, Nanny's soups were broth-based, simple concoctions. Most of all, they were great ways to enjoy the bounty of the Houghton Ranch.

A TYPICAL DAY

AT THE PENS

H O T

CORN CHOWDER

Corn grew wonderfully well at the Ranch. In spite of the deer and raccoons that raided the fields almost nightly, there was lots of fresh corn and Nanny enjoyed serving it several ways. This corn chowder is inspired by a spicy version of creamed corn that I remember but for which I could find no recipe. Following Nanny's penchant for flavoring with bacon, onion, and hot pepper, this chowder was conceived with her typical proportions and then laced with pepper and mild ground chile to torch it in the southwestern style. I think Nanny would have been pleased. It's a hearty soup; if it strikes you as a bit too thick, just add more milk to taste.

METHOD

Fry the bacon until crisp, remove from the pan and drain on paper towels. Pour off all but 2 tablespoons of the bacon drippings.

Sauté the green pepper and onions in the bacon drippings until the onions are golden.

Place the potatoes and the water in a large saucepan, add the pepper and onion mixture, the salt, and pepper, bring to a boil and simmer for 10 minutes.

While the potatoes are simmering, melt the butter in another saucepan, add the flour, and stir until smooth. Add the milk, bring to a boil, stirring, and simmer for 5 minutes; take care not to let the mixture scorch. Add the ground chiles or paprika and stir until smooth.

Stir the milk mixture into the potato mixture and mix well. Stir in the cream and corn. Crumble the bacon and stir in. Simmer the chowder for 10 minutes, correct the seasoning, and serve hot.

INGREDIENTS

- 1/4 pound smoked bacon, thickly sliced
- 1 small green pepper, cut into 1/4" dice
- 2 medium onions, cut into 1/4" dice
- 3/4 pound boiling potatoes, peeled and cut into 1/4" dice
- 2 cups water
- 1/2 teaspoon salt or to taste
- 1/2 teaspoon pepper
- 3 tablespoons butter
- 3 tablespoons flour
- 2 cups milk
- 1/2 teaspoon mild ground chiles or paprika
- 1/2 cup heavy cream
- 2 1/2 cups fresh corn kernels, or 2 10-ounce packages frozen corn, thawed

YIELD · 2 QUARTS · 6–8 SERVINGS

ONION SOUP

The mild, savory flavor of this surprisingly light soup reminds me of the onions grown at the Ranch—so sweet and mild, I've heard more than one visitor remark, "Why, you could eat these onions like apples!" Unlike many recipes for onion soup, this one calls for chicken stock rather than beef and features, of all things, fennel. The result is a light, almost "buttery" broth that's "oniony" sweet and "finished" or savoried with a hint of licorice flavor from the fennel. Never mind the clinical analysis, though. Just try it, and see if this doesn't change your conception of what makes good onion soup. This recipe makes a lot of soup, and can be halved, if desired.

INGREDIENTS

- *4 tablespoons butter*
- *4 tablespoons vegetable oil*
- *4 pounds medium to large onions, thinly sliced*
- *1 clove garlic, minced*
- *4 quarts homemade or canned chicken broth (see note)*
- *1 teaspoon salt or to taste*
- *1 teaspoon pepper or to taste*
- *2 tablespoons fresh fennel tops, chopped, or 1 tablespoon fennel seeds*
- *1 cup dry sherry or vermouth*
- *16 ½"-thick slices of French bread*
- *shredded or sliced Gruyère or grated Parmesan cheese*

METHOD

In a very large frying pan, heat the butter and oil and sauté the onions and garlic until transparent. Bring the chicken broth to a boil in a large kettle. Add the onions and garlic, the salt, pepper, and fennel and simmer partially covered for 30 to 40 minutes. Add sherry or vermouth and correct the seasonings.

Lightly toast the sliced bread.

To serve, ladle the soup into individual bowls. Top with the toasted French bread, sprinkle with cheese, and run under a hot broiler until the cheese is browned and bubbly.

NOTE: *If using canned broth, the salt in this recipe should be omitted, as commercially processed broth is highly salted.*

YIELD · 4 QUARTS · 16 SERVINGS

SAGEBRUSH SOUP

The silvery pea-green color of this delicious game soup reminds me of the range in early spring. The flavors and aroma, though, are redolent of roast prairie chicken or pheasant. Heady with sage, the broth is laced with garlic, sour cream, and sherry. As for the meat, it takes on an almost buttery taste. It's enough to make you want to roast a bird just to make the soup!

METHOD

In a large pot bring the water to a boil; add the frame(s), reduce heat, and simmer until the meat falls off the bones. Strain the stock into a bowl. Pick any remaining meat off the bones, dice, and set aside. You should have at least 1 cup of meat.

Return the stock to the pot and add the thyme, sage, and vegetables. Simmer until the vegetables are very tender. Strain the stock again into a bowl and force the vegetables through a strainer or puree in a blender or food processor. Return the stock and pureed vegetables to the pot and blend well. Heat to the simmering point. Stir in the sour cream and sherry and blend well, but do not boil. Correct the seasoning. Add the meat.

Ladle into soup bowls and serve garnished with a dollop of sour cream or croutons, and sprinkled with parsley.

YIELD · ABOUT 1¾ QUARTS
6−8 SERVINGS

INGREDIENTS

1 pheasant frame, or 2 chicken frames, cooked

2 quarts water

½ teaspoon dried thyme

½ teaspoon dried ground sage, or 1 teaspoon minced fresh

1 onion, chopped

3 carrots, peeled, thinly sliced

2 stalks celery with leaves, sliced

¾ pound boiling potatoes, peeled and sliced

¼ cup sour cream, room temperature

¼ cup dry sherry

Salt and pepper to taste

GARNISH:

Sour cream or croutons
Chopped fresh parsley

WINTER GAME SOUP

Don't throw out the frames from your prairie chicken or pheasant. They make the stock that goes into this hearty winter broth. Parsnips, potatoes, carrots, and onions or leeks combine well with the gamy stock to produce a creamy soup that's quite elegant when laced with sweet white wine or vermouth. If you like a thicker soup, increase the flour and butter to taste, or puree some of the cooked vegetables and combine with the specified amounts of butter and flour. The addition of a lettuce leaf is an old Flemish custom that adds color and the taste of something fresh and green.

INGREDIENTS

- 2 *quarts water*
- 1 *pheasant frame, or 2 chicken frames, cooked*
- 2 *stalks celery with leaves, cut into 1" pieces*
- 1 *medium onion, or 2 leeks, cut into 1" pieces*
- 1 *garlic clove, minced*
- 2 *bay leaves*
- 4 *tablespoons butter*
- 4 *tablespoons flour*
- 1 *teaspoon salt*
- 1/2 *teaspoon pepper*
- 1 *teaspoon dried leaf sage, ground*
- 3 *carrots, peeled, cut into 1" pieces*
- 2 *parsnips, peeled, cut into 1" pieces*
- 1 *pound boiling potatoes, peeled and cubed*
- 1 *cup heavy cream*
- 3 *tablespoons sweet white wine or dry vermouth*

GARNISH:

- 1 *small head Boston lettuce, leaves separated and washed*

METHOD

In a large pot bring the water to a boil, add the frame(s), celery, onion, garlic, and bay leaves; reduce heat and simmer until the meat falls off the bones. Strain the stock into a bowl; reserve the vegetables, if desired. Pick any remaining meat off the bones and set aside. You should have at least 1 cup of meat.

In a large saucepan or soup pot, melt the butter and stir in the flour until smooth. Pour in the stock and stir until smooth. Add the salt, pepper, and sage and heat to boiling. Add the carrots, parsnips, and potatoes and simmer until just tender. Return the reserved celery and onions to the soup, if desired, along with the meat. Add the cream and simmer for a few minutes.

Just before serving, add the wine and correct the seasoning if necessary. Ladle into soup bowls and garnish each bowl with a lettuce leaf.

YIELD · 2 ½ QUARTS · 8 SERVINGS

COLD

GAZPACHO

There's nothing quite like this Andalusian ambrosia in late summer. This cold, festive soup is certainly at its best when the tomatoes, peppers, and onions at the Ranch are at their zenith. In this version, which is adapted from a recipe by Helen Witty that Nanny saved from the August 1964 issue of *The Flower Grower*, chopped cilantro and ground cumin make the flavors of the fresh vegetables pop like they do in a good bowl of "red." For more color and sweeter flavor, you can substitute sweet red pepper. As for serving suggestions, a bowl of gazpacho with Nanny's Enchilada Stack make a great Tex-Mex "soup and sandwich."

METHOD

Place the garlic in a large bowl. Peel, core, and seed the tomatoes, placing the seeds in a colander over a bowl and pressing the juices out. Save the juices. Press the tomatoes through a coarse sieve or food mill, or puree in a food processor. Add to the garlic, along with the tomato-seed juices. Stir in the olive oil, drop by drop, until well blended.

Add the pepper, onion, and cucumbers to the tomato mixture. Add the paprika, salt, cumin, and vinegar. Stir in the crumbs and the water. Taste and adjust the seasonings if necessary. Chill.

Serve topped with the chopped parsley or cilantro.

YIELD · 2½ QUARTS · 8–10 SERVINGS

INGREDIENTS

1 clove garlic, minced

6–8 large tomatoes

3–4 tablespoons olive oil

1 large green pepper, seeded, deveined, and minced

1 large sweet onion, minced

2 cucumbers, peeled, seeded, and minced

1 teaspoon paprika

1 teaspoon salt

3/4–1 teaspoon ground cumin

2–3 tablespoons wine vinegar

1/4 cup fresh white bread crumbs

2½ cups cold water

GARNISH:

1–2 tablespoons chopped fresh parsley or cilantro

ICED CUCUMBER SOUP

INGREDIENTS

3 *large cucumbers, peeled, seeded, and sliced*

3–4 *slices of mild onion, or 2 scallions, white part only, sliced*

3 *tablespoons butter*

3 *tablespoons flour*

1 *quart homemade or canned chicken broth*

Salt

White pepper

½ *cup heavy cream*

GARNISH:

Chopped fresh dill, chives, or tarragon

Summers on the High Plains get hot, to say the least—104 degrees in the shade during July and August is not uncommon. Iced Cucumber Soup served at supper, is a cool and soothing reward for getting through the day.

Nanny collected this soup recipe also from the August 1964 issue of *The Flower Grower*. It is light and creamy, but its texture and saltiness will be affected by the kind of chicken broth used. Commercial or powdered broth will be saltier; homemade will be much thicker. Also, it's important to use firm, fresh cucumbers. As for seasoning the soup, it should be done just before serving because the flavors are diminished by the chilling.

METHOD

In a large saucepan heat the butter; add the cucumbers and onion or scallions. Sauté very slowly for 10 minutes. Stir in the flour until smooth. Add the chicken broth and bring to a simmer, stirring constantly until smooth. Season with salt and pepper to taste, and simmer for 15 minutes. Puree in a blender, food mill, or food processor until silky smooth. Add the cream and taste for seasonings. Chill. Retaste for seasonings.

Serve sprinkled with chopped dill, chives or tarragon.

YIELD · 1 ¼ CUPS · 4–6 SERVINGS

VICHYSSOISE

Ted Houghton loved vichyssoise. When my mother came to visit, she'd make her recipe by the gallon, much to his delight. This version makes about 2 quarts. It's thick with potatoes and heady with herbs, and is just as nice served hot. Of course, if it's hot, it's not vichyssoise, just good hot potato soup. Uncle Ted, "Unc" for short, relished it served either way.

M E T H O D

Place the chicken broth in a large kettle. Add the potatoes to the broth. Cut the leeks into ¼″ slices, using all the white part and a little of the green, and add to the broth. Add the onions. Season with the salt, pepper, parsley, and dill and bring all to a simmer. Simmer for 30 minutes, or until the vegetables are soft.

Cool the soup to lukewarm. Puree in batches in a blender or food processor until smooth. Chill.

When ready to serve, add the cream and stir in thoroughly. Correct the seasonings. Serve in chilled bowls with a sprinkling of chives as garnish.

NOTE: *If using canned broth do not add salt until last and season to taste as commercially processed broth is highly salted.*

Especially after chilling, the soup may be too thick; thin with milk if necessary in addition to the cream to the desired consistency.

YIELD · 2 QUARTS · ABOUT 8 SERVINGS

INGREDIENTS

6 cups homemade or canned chicken broth

2 pounds potatoes, peeled and sliced

6 leeks, washed and trimmed

2 medium onions, sliced

½ teaspoon salt

½ teaspoon pepper

2 tablespoons chopped fresh parsley

2 tablespoons chopped fresh dill

1 cup light cream

GARNISH:

Chopped fresh chives

WEEKEND GUESTS
''COMIN' HOME FOR
DINNER''

SALADS, MOLDS, AND DRESSINGS

Whether it's incredibly hot or incredibly cold, it's always incredibly dry on the High Plains. It's so dry, they joke, even the rain's dry! It might as well be. On average, the Ranch receives less than eighteen inches of rainfall per year.

Yet, even a little water will make anything grow in this area's gray, sandy loam. Ultimately, a big spring irrigates everything inside the oasis —man, beast, fruits, vegetables, and, of course, just about anything that goes into the salads served at the Ranch. Until the 100-degree heat of midsummer makes it "bolt" (or shoot up), wonderfully tender leaf lettuce is raised at the Ranch with careful irrigation. To add to the variety, the "Big Spring" yields some of the most delicate watercress I've eaten anywhere. Watercress is tossed into salad and used as a garnish for clever dishes such as whole tomato aspic. Then, there's Nanny's fabulous, famous Wilted Lettuce Salad. The variety is tantalizing.

Warm and pungent wilted lettuce, cool and sweet carrot and pineapple, briny cucumber, juicy tomatoes with sweet white onion, and peppery garlic beans represent the spectrum of flavors found in the salads mentioned in this chapter. Add to this a Mexican-style avocado dressing, an old-time Lone Star favorite called "ambrosia," or a tart German potato salad and you'll get an idea of the ethnic backgrounds at work on Nanny's Texas table.

FOOTBRIDGE
OVER THE
ROMERO CREEK,
HARRIET
KRITSER,
1930

SALADS

AMBROSIA

This "old-timey" Texan recipe dates back to the days when fresh citrus or tropical fruits were a novelty in cattle country, and refrigeration, even by ice, hardly existed. Anything made with oranges and coconut was considered a delicacy. Indeed, Nanny and her mother remembered those pioneer days well and considered Ambrosia a rare treat long after oranges and coconut became as common as apples and pears.

METHOD

Place one-quarter of the orange sections and apple slices in a serving bowl. Sprinkle with a quarter of the pecans and the coconut. Drizzle with 1 tablespoon orange juice. Repeat, making 4 layers in all. Refrigerate until serving time.

VARIATION: *1 or 2 tablespoonfuls of rum or orange-flavored liqueur may be drizzled over the Ambrosia just before serving.*

YIELD · 6 SERVINGS

INGREDIENTS

- 4 large navel oranges, peeled and sectioned
- 2 large Golden or Red Delicious apples, peeled, cored, and sliced
- ½ cup chopped pecans
- 1 cup fresh or canned shredded coconut
- 4 tablespoons orange juice

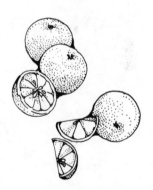

CUCUMBER AND ONION IN VINEGAR AND BRINE

INGREDIENTS

- *1 large (8″ long) cucumber, peeled and sliced*
- *1 small onion, sliced, separated into rings*
- *1 cup water*
- *2 tablespoons white vinegar*
- *¼ tablespoon pepper*
- *½ tablespoon salt*

As long as they're in season, there's always a covered glass dish of cucumbers and onions soaking in brine in the old Puffer-Hubbard refrigerator at the Headquarters. Generously spiked with pepper, the brine itself takes on the onion and cucumber flavors to make a refreshingly light dressing for sliced tomatoes. For additional color and interest, thin-sliced radishes mix quite well with the cucumber and onion.

METHOD

Mix the cucumber and onion slices together in a bowl. Combine the remaining ingredients and pour over the cucumber and onion. Refrigerate overnight, stirring occasionally. It will keep a week.

YIELD · 2 CUPS

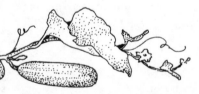

GERMAN POTATO SALAD

Smoked bacon, sweet onions, and tart cider vinegar make this version of German potato salad a sweet-sour complement to rich meats or game.

METHOD

Place the potatoes in a pot, cover with water, and bring to a boil. Boil for 20 to 30 minutes, or until tender.

While the potatoes are cooking, cut the bacon into small pieces and fry until crisp. Remove the bacon bits with a slotted spoon and drain on paper towels. Reserve the grease in the frying pan.

When the potatoes are cooked, drain, reserving a cup of the cooking water. When cool enough to handle, peel the potatoes and slice. Place in a large serving bowl. Add the diced onion and eggs to the potato slices.

Place the frying pan with bacon grease over heat. Add the vinegar, sugar, and reserved potato water and bring to a boil. Simmer for 1 minute, then pour over the potato slices. Add the salt, pepper, and bacon pieces. Toss to blend well. Sprinkle with parsley and serve warm.

YIELD · 2½ QUARTS 10 OR MORE SERVINGS

INGREDIENTS

4 pounds white boiling potatoes, washed

½ pound smoked bacon

1 medium onion, diced

4 eggs, hard-cooked and diced

½ cup cider vinegar

1 tablespoon sugar

1 cup potato cooking water

2 teaspoons salt

1 teaspoon pepper

GARNISH:

2 tablespoons chopped fresh parsley

GARLIC BEANS

Whether you serve them as a salad or condiment, these garlic beans are a terrific complement to spare ribs or barbecue. A little sweeter than green beans vinaigrette, they're laced with more garlic than three bean salad. These beans are also quite nice with tuna salad or for turning out a quick salad niçoise.

METHOD

If using canned beans, rinse and drain. Layer the beans with the onion slices in a 1-quart dish. Sprinkle each layer with some of the garlic salt and pepper. Mix the olive oil, vinegar, and sugar together and pour over all. Place in the refrigerator and let stand overnight. Serve cold.

YIELD · 1 QUART · 4–6 SERVINGS

INGREDIENTS

1 pound fresh green beans, blanched, or 2 cans whole green beans

1 small onion, thinly sliced

¾–1 teaspoon garlic salt

¼ teaspoon pepper

½ cup olive oil

¾ cup vinegar, preferably cider vinegar

3 tablespoons sugar

POTATO SALAD

Young new potatoes with their waxy red skins left on, and fresh dill make this potato salad taste "fresh from the garden." Add a touch of onion, if you like, but be sure to use *real* mayonnaise—not salad dressing. Any of the sweeter "salad dressings" will not produce the same light salad.

INGREDIENTS

1 *pound small new or red potatoes*

½ *cup mayonnaise*

1 *tablespoon chopped fresh dill*

1 *tablespoon chopped fresh parsley*

1 *green pepper, chopped*

2 *eggs, hard-cooked and chopped*

1 *teaspoon salt*

1½ *teaspoons pepper*

GARNISH:

Paprika

METHOD

Boil the potatoes until just tender. Drain, cool, and quarter. Toss gently but thoroughly with all the remaining ingredients. Add more mayonnaise, if necessary. Sprinkle with paprika and chill until serving time.

YIELD · 3 CUPS · 4 SERVINGS

WILTED LETTUCE

If there's a salad for which Martha Houghton is remembered, it's her Wilted Lettuce. I can't recall my father ever speaking of dinner at the Ranch without fondly mentioning "Martha's Wilted Lettuce." It's a perennial favorite at the Ranch, and the recipe has been generously handed down through the years. The recipe printed here was derived from a demonstration by Nanny's granddaughter Lisa Morton. Somehow it was never written down until now—just passed along verbally from one enthusiastic cook to another. If you wish, you can substitute spinach for the lettuce.

INGREDIENTS

- 2 heads Boston or salad-bowl lettuce, washed and dried
- 2 scallions, thinly sliced
- ¾ pound bacon strips
- 1½ tablespoons sugar
- 1¼ teaspoons yellow, prepared "salad" mustard
- 2 tablespoons cider vinegar

METHOD

Tear or cut the lettuce into 2″ strips and place in a bowl. Add the scallions to the lettuce.

Fry the bacon until crisp. Crumble and add to the lettuce. Drain off the bacon grease and return ⅓ cup of grease to the pan. Let it cool a bit, so as not to caramelize the sugar, then add the sugar and stir to dissolve, while gently scraping the pan. Add the mustard and then the vinegar, and stir to mix well. Bring to a boil and pour immediately over the lettuce, bacon, and scallions. Toss well and serve immediately.

YIELD · 4–6 SERVINGS

MOLDS

NANNY'S CRANBERRY JELLY RING

During the 1920s, Nanny must have become quite interested in recipes that called for natural gelatin. As I combed through her collection of recipes and household notes, I found any number of salads or preparations that called for "acidulated" gelatin scribbled on file cards, backs of envelopes, shopping lists, or handy scraps of paper. This one cleverly turns ordinary, home-cooked cranberries into a shimmering mold that, when unmolded, produces clear, claret-colored gelatin over barely popped cranberries. It's a great way to satisfy fans of cranberry jelly and whole-berry sauce at once. Besides the obvious roasted turkey, this cranberry mold is also quite nice with wild fowl such as mallard duck or Canada goose.

INGREDIENTS

- 2 *cups sugar*
- 1 *cup water*
- *Zest of 1 orange, cut into slivers*
- 1 *package fresh cranberries*
- 1½ *envelopes of unflavored gelatin*
- ¼ *cup cold water*

METHOD

Combine the sugar and water in a large saucepan. Add the slivers of zest and bring all to a boil. Stir in the cranberries and cook until the berries pop, about 5 minutes.

Meanwhile, soften the gelatin in the cold water. Rinse a 4-cup ring mold with cold water.

Remove the berries from the heat and stir in the softened gelatin, stirring until the gelatin dissolves. Pour into the rinsed mold and chill until firm, at least 6 hours. Unmold before serving.

YIELD · 8–16 SERVINGS

WHOLE TOMATO ASPIC

Martha Houghton loved tomatoes and finding new ways to add interest to her favorite recipes. Here, the standard aspic calls for whole canned tomatoes and chopped green pepper. It's a pleasant variation and adds a pleasing texture as well as a festive appearance to the molded aspic.

METHOD

Place the tomatoes, onion, pepper, sugar, and salt in a saucepan. Bring to a boil and simmer for 10 minutes. As the mixture is cooking, break up the tomatoes into roughly 1-inch cubes with the side of a spoon.

Soften the gelatin in the cold water. Rinse a 4-cup ring mold or eight ½-cup individual molds with cold water.

When the tomatoes are cooked, add the gelatin and stir to dissolve. Pour into the wet mold(s) and chill until set. Serve on a bed of lettuce.

YIELD · 8 SERVINGS

INGREDIENTS

1 *28-ounce can whole tomatoes, undrained*

2 *tablespoons minced onion*

¼ *cup chopped green pepper*

1 *tablespoon sugar*

1 *teaspoon salt*

2 *envelopes of unflavored gelatin*

½ *cup cold water*

Lettuce leaves

CARROT-PINEAPPLE SALAD

2 *cups unsweetened pineapple juice*

1 *envelope of unflavored gelatin, 3 tablespoons sugar, and 1 tablespoon lemon juice, combined, or 1 package lemon Jell-O*

1 *cup mayonnaise*

2 *cups grated carrots*

1 *20-ounce can unsweetened crushed pineapple, drained*

Sunday supper at the Ranch was the next best thing to an icebox raid. The help was off and we'd all pile into the kitchen to build sky-high sandwiches from a week's worth of incredible, edible leftovers. Anything that could be enjoyed cold was brought out of the huge, double-doored Puffer-Hubbard refrigerator with stout enameled legs and tremendous chrome handles. (Actually, this fridge might as well have been called the "Hummer-Hubbard" for its constant high-pitched vibrations.) When ham was served for Sunday supper, having this delicious salad with it was a long-standing tradition. In fact, it continued to be served as a favorite side dish long after gelatin-based recipes passed out of fashion.

This recipe calls for using a decorative dish. For an elegant touch, try a white soufflé dish. The top of the salad will jell to a creamy hue, and the shredded carrots will dot the surface in subtle contrast.

METHOD

In a large saucepan heat the pineapple juice until hot. Stir in the unflavored gelatin mixture or the Jell-O until dissolved. Let the mixture cool until barely warm. Stir in the mayonnaise and blend thoroughly. Stir in the carrots and pineapple and mix well. Pour into a 6-cup decorative serving dish and chill until set.

NOTE: *For a sweeter version, use canned pineapple in heavy syrup.*

YIELD · 12 SERVINGS

DRESSINGS

"SUNNY" SALAD DRESSING

Don't throw out your leftover juice from Nanny's Pickled Summer Squash. It makes a great addition to salad dressing or cole slaw!

METHOD

Marinate the chopped pecans in the honey and garlic for 2 hours. Mix the juice, vinegar, mustard, and salt and pepper well. Whisk in the olive oil, then the vegetable oil, a few drops at a time until creamy. If using a blender, add oils in a thin, steady stream at low speed.

NOTE: *If you have no juice from Nanny's Pickled Summer Squash, you may substitute 2 tablespoons cider vinegar, ¼ teaspoon mustard seed, and ¼ teaspoon celery seed.*

YIELD · 1 ½ CUPS

INGREDIENTS

2 tablespoons chopped pecans

1 tablespoon honey

1 clove garlic, minced

2 tablespoons pickled squash juice from Nanny's Pickled Yellow Squash (page 59) (see Note)

1 tablespoon cider vinegar

1 teaspoon Dijon mustard

1 level teaspoon salt

½ teaspoon pepper

3 tablespoons olive oil

3 tablespoons vegetable oil

AVOCADO DRESSING

INGREDIENTS

- ½ cup Guacamole (page 139)
- 3 tablespoons lime juice
- 1 teaspoon dry mustard
- ½ teaspoon sugar
- ¼ teaspoon ground coriander
- 9 tablespoons olive oil
- 1–2 teaspoons Gar's Chili Salsa (page 181)

Salads with Tex-Mex ingredients beg for avocados and the juice of sweet, tart limes. This piquant dressing combines spicy guacamole with a simple lime juice vinaigrette to make a creamy dressing perfect for a salad of lettuce and tomatoes. If you need to feed a "posse" inexpensively, try a big salad with this dressing and a casserole of baked Enchiladas con Queso.

METHOD

Place the guacamole in a bowl. Stir in the lime juice, mustard, sugar, and coriander until well mixed. Whisk in the olive oil, a little at a time, and add the chili salsa to taste.

YIELD · APPROXIMATELY 1 ¼ CUPS

BEEFSTEAK DRESSING

INGREDIENTS

- 1 cup mayonnaise
- 1 clove garlic, minced
- 1 teaspoon Worcestershire sauce
- 2 teaspoons chopped scallions
- ½ teaspoon dry mustard
- ½ teaspoon sugar
  Pinch ground cumin
- ¾ cup beef broth or bouillon
  Salt and pepper to taste

When they were in season, Nanny rarely served dinner without a platter of thick-sliced beefsteak tomatoes. We never tired of them, though, when eaten with dressings like this one. In spite of its relatively thin consistency, this dressing is quite good with salads composed of delicate leaf lettuce. It's also quite nice on salads garnished with chopped hard-cooked eggs.

METHOD

In a small bowl, blend the mayonnaise, garlic, Worcestershire, scallions, mustard, sugar, and cumin; mix well, then slowly add the bouillon, stirring all the while. Add salt and pepper to taste. Refrigerate until ready to use.

YIELD · ALMOST 2 CUPS

P I C K L E S
A N D
PRESERVES

The first settler known to inhabit
the oasis which came to be the center of activities for the Houghton
Ranch was one Dolores Duran. As
a homesteader in the mid-1870s,
she must have been a hearty soul.
In those days, there was more to
contend with than just harsh
weather and little rain; there were
Indians.

It is unclear when she arrived,
but in 1874, and just seventy-five
miles away from the oasis, twenty-
eight buffalo hunters and traders,

with one brave woman, had to defend themselves against an extended assault by seven hundred Indians at the now-famous "Adobe Walls." The Anglos won, but the humiliated tribes went on a rampage. They fanned out over the High Plains and for two months ravaged the land, killing almost two hundred whites. The region was considered so unsafe that three more years passed before the first cattleman would graze his herd in the Panhandle.

Somehow, Dolores Duran succeeded in spite of the weather, lack of rain, and the proximity of hostile Indians. She planted fruit trees, tilled the sandy loam, and irrigated with creek water that flowed down from the Big Spring three miles away. By the time two drovers from Colorado named Lee and Reynolds brought the first herd of cattle to the Romero Canyon in 1879, they found a house "well developed, in a picturesque setting of garden, orchard, and flowers." So, fruits and vegetables probably have been picked or preserved even longer than cattle have been pastured at the Ranch.

In earlier times, what couldn't be eaten fresh had to be "put by" for the barren winter. Fruits and vegetables were "put up" to be sweet, sour, or pungent, and later served with hot, spicy meat that could be a bit "off" or gamy from the lack of refrigeration. There was no lack of imagination, though. Some great recipes and serving combinations have survived long past this necessity: Candied Sweet Pickles with barbecue, Mustard Pickle with ham, pickled Dilly Beans with cold roast beef, and pickled okra with just about anything. Green Tomato Mincemeat was served like chutney or used in tarts and pies. And of course, jams and jellies were served with biscuits and such. Those offered here are old-fashioned favorites; others are clever variations, but most are still put up and enjoyed at the Ranch.

PICKLES

CANDIED SWEET PICKLES

Sliced dill pickles take on a whole new identity with this quick, clever recipe. The cinnamon and cloves in the pickling spices produce a sharp, clean taste that's especially complementary to smoked ham and, even without the ham, almost addictive. You can cut the ingredients in half and make it by the pint, but if you put up the whole quart you'll be glad you did.

INGREDIENTS

1 quart dill pickles, sliced
2½ cups sugar
½ cup cider vinegar
3 tablespoons pickling spice

METHOD

Drain the pickles and return to the jar.

In a saucepan bring the remaining ingredients to a boil and heat until the sugar is dissolved. Pour the mixture over the pickles and let cool. Refrigerate for at least 3 days before serving.

YIELD · 1 QUART

DILLY BEANS (OR CARROTS)

Crisp and crunchy, these unusual sweet pickles are great partners with cold roast beef or ham. As the recipe indicates, you can make them with dillseed or dillweed. The dillseed imparts a slight aniselike flavor, the weed more what we associate with sour dill. For colorful variety, try carrots.

INGREDIENTS

*1 pound green beans,
washed and
trimmed, or 2
pounds carrots,
peeled and cut into
1/2"-x-2" strips*

1 cup cider vinegar

1 cup sugar

*1 tablespoon dried
dillweed or dillseed*

*Salt and pepper to
taste*

METHOD

Cut any long green beans in half if desired.

Bring enough water to cover the beans or carrots to a boil; add the vegetable and boil for 2 to 3 minutes. Drain, saving 1 cup of the cooking water.

Mix the water with the vinegar and sugar, add the beans or carrots, and return the pan to the stove. Bring to a boil, cover, remove from heat, and allow to cool.

Add the dill, correct seasoning, and place beans or carrots in a glass or ceramic container. Refrigerate overnight before using. The beans or carrots will keep for 3 to 4 weeks if refrigerated.

YIELD · 1 QUART

MUSTARD PICKLE

INGREDIENTS

1 cup salt

1 gallon water

3–4 cucumbers, sliced

4 onions, sliced

*4 stalks celery,
sliced*

*4 green tomatoes,
cored and diced*

*1 head cauliflower,
separated into
florets*

*2 green peppers,
seeded and diced*

*1 quart cider
vinegar*

*2 tablespoons
Colman's English
dry mustard*

(continued)

Nanny and my mother, Pauline Ross, corresponded at least once or twice a month for decades. Recipes along with family news were no doubt "staples," and this one for Mustard Pickle turned up in Mother's handwriting among Nanny's vast collection of recipes for pickles and preserves. This version of mustard pickle is particularly tart and calls for a full charge of Colman's English mustard powder. At the Ranch, these pickles were most frequently served with ham, but they would be equally appealing with venison, antelope, or meat loaf.

METHOD

Make a brine with the water and salt. Mix together the vegetables with the brine and soak overnight, or for at least 12 hours.

The next morning drain the vegetables thoroughly, place in a pot, cover with fresh water, and bring to a boil. Cook until barely tender.

Meanwhile, make a dressing by adding 2 cups vinegar to the mustard, sugar, flour, and seasonings, mixing well. In a separate pan bring the remaining 2 cups vinegar to a boil, stir in the mustard mixture, and bring the whole thing to a boil.

Drain the vegetables and pour the dressing over them. Preserve according to proper canning techniques.

YIELD · 3 ½ QUARTS

1 cup sugar

½ cup all-purpose flour

1 tablespoon turmeric

½ teaspoon curry powder

½ tablespoon ground ginger

⅛ teaspoon cayenne

PICKLED BEETS

The best way to introduce these sweet-sour beets is to quote Martha Houghton from the recipe she jotted down on the back of an envelope: "Try these—good."

M E T H O D

Trim the beets, leaving 2-inch stems. Put in a saucepan with water to cover, bring to a boil, and boil until tender, 15 to 25 minutes. Drain and peel the beets and place in a pint jar.

In another saucepan bring the sugar and vinegar to a boil and pour over the beets. Store in the refrigerator or preserve according to proper canning techniques.

NOTE: *If you like pickled eggs, the beet juice from this recipe is terrific for adding flavor and color to peeled, hard-cooked eggs. It takes about a day in the refrigerator to make the eggs turn lavender and piquant. If you really want to go for the whole Ranch, try these eggs deviled. The few minutes it takes to mash and mix the yolks with mayonnaise, dry mustard, and a little Worcestershire is well worth it. A drop or two of Tabasco won't slow you down either!*

YIELD · 1 PINT · QUANTITIES MAY BE INCREASED AS LONG AS SYRUP IS MADE OF EQUAL PARTS OF SUGAR AND VINEGAR.

INGREDIENTS

2 bunches small to medium beets (8–10 beets), washed

1 cup sugar

1 cup cider vinegar

PICKLED PEACHES

INGREDIENTS

- 4 *pounds ripe peaches*
- 1 *pint cider vinegar*
- 3 *cups sugar*
- ½ *teaspoon ground cloves*
- ½ *teaspoon ground cinnamon*
- ½ *teaspoon ground ginger*

The peaches that grow at the Ranch are unlike any I have ever tasted. When ripe and eaten right from the tree, they're warm from the sun and bursting with sweet, sweet juice at first bite. Pickled this way, the peaches take on a sharp snap and a slightly nutty, almondlike flavor that makes them a savory condiment at meals that feature pork or dark-meat fowl such as duck or goose.

METHOD

Cut up 1 peach. In a large pot mix the peach, the vinegar, sugar, and spices. Bring to a boil; boil for 30 minutes, and strain.

Return the syrup to the pot. When the syrup is boiling, bring a pot of water to a boil and drop the whole peaches in for 1 minute. Remove and skin the peaches. Add the peaches to the strained syrup and boil them for 5 to 10 minutes, until you can just pierce them with a knife. Do not overcook the peaches.

Put the peaches into sterilized jars and pour the boiling syrup over them. Preserve according to proper canning methods.

YIELD · 3 QUARTS

PICKLED YELLOW SQUASH

The notion of bringing Nanny's recipe for sweet pickles together with one of her favorite vegetables led to this recipe. Since crops of home-grown squash inevitably exceed demand, this is a tantalizing way to save some choice, young pieces. Squash is easy to put up and maintains its bright yellow color and crunchy flavor quite well. For variety, serve the squash anywhere you like sweet pickles. For an interesting salad, finely dice some pickled squash and onions. Then toss into a mixed green salad with French, Russian, or creamy Italian dressing.

INGREDIENTS

6 *medium yellow squash, washed and cut into 1/4" slices (about 2 pounds)*

1 *red pepper, seeded, deveined, and cut into 1/4" dice*

2 *medium onions, cut into 1/4" slices, then separated into rings*

1/4 *cup kosher salt*

2 *cups white vinegar*

2 *cups sugar*

2 *teaspoons mustard seed*

2 *teaspoons celery seed*

METHOD

Place the squash, red pepper, and onions in a large glass bowl. Sprinkle with the salt and toss to mix well. Pour on enough cold water to cover, place a plate on top to keep the slices submerged, and let stand for 2 hours.

Drain the squash and onions, rinse, and drain well.

In a large pot combine the vinegar, sugar, mustard seed, and celery seed. Boil for 2 minutes, add the drained squash, red pepper, and onions, and cook for 5 minutes, but do not boil. Cool and refrigerate or preserve according to proper canning methods.

YIELD · 4 PINTS

GREEN TOMATO MINCEMEAT

Green tomatoes find their way to the table at the Ranch several different ways, but this recipe for mincemeat is the most unusual. Mincemeat traditionally calls for suet, chopped beef or ox heart, and nuts. This one—found in the 1928 *Woman's Club of Fort Worth Cookbook* and dedicated to Nanny's aunt, Anna Shelton, who was president of the Club at the time—does not, using chopped green tomatoes and more raisins than usual in their place. The result is exceptionally pungent, and without the suet, clearly lower in cholesterol.

For pies or tarts, add a shot or two of brandy or bourbon. Or, try it alone as a condiment for stronger game such as goose or venison.

INGREDIENTS

- 4 medium to large green tomatoes, cored and chopped
- 4 medium to large apples, peeled, cored, and chopped
- 3 cups light or dark brown sugar
- 4 tablespoons butter
- 1 pound golden or dark raisins
- 1 teaspooon ground cloves
- 1 teaspoon ground cinnamon
- 1 cup cider vinegar

METHOD

Mix all the ingredients together in a pot and simmer for 2 hours, or until thick. Cool and refrigerate, or preserve according to proper canning techniques.

YIELD · 1 ½ QUARTS

PRESERVES

JAM, ESPECIALLY APRICOT

This recipe will make a good, relatively soft jam from almost any fruit that has enough natural pectin, such as peaches, plums, or strawberries. Personally, I like what it does for apricots best. Even "store-bought" apricots out of season give this jam a sunny, orangey glow.

Several varieties of apricots are raised at the Ranch, but the ones I remember best grow on huge, spreading trees in an orchard halfway between the Headquarters and the lakes. When the apricots are ripe, it's great fun to ride by on horseback and pick off some perfect fruit for a perfect snack. Even though it's been quite a while since I've picked an apricot while seated on the back of a horse, a spoonful of jam made with Nanny's recipe never fails to take me back.

INGREDIENTS

4 *cups sugar*

7 *tablespoons water*

4 *cups fruit (apricots, peaches, plums, or strawberries)*

METHOD

In a 6- or 8-quart saucepan or kettle mix the sugar and water and bring slowly to a full boil, about 200°F on a candy thermometer. Stir in the fruit thoroughly and bring to a brisk boil. Let it boil for 7 to 10 minutes. If the jam boils for the full 10 minutes, it will be thicker than if it boils for 7 minutes. Pour the jam into crocks or jars and let stand overnight. Cap when cold and keep refrigerated. The jam can keep up to 10 months in the refrigerator, that is, if it isn't eaten up first!

YIELD · 1 ¼ QUARTS

PLUM JELLY

Plums vary greatly in tartness and ripeness. The ones that grow wild at the Ranch are very small, Chinese red, tart, and hard. The jelly Nanny made was tart and slightly runny. An equally excellent jelly can be made by using other plum varieties.

INGREDIENTS

8 pounds plums (see Note), washed and cut up, pits reserved

2 cups water

3 cups sugar

Pectin, if needed

METHOD

Place the plum pits in a large cooking pot with a lid. Crush the cut-up plum flesh or chop finely in a food processor. Add to the pits in the pot. Add the water, cover, and bring to a boil. Simmer, covered, for 10 to 15 minutes, stirring occasionally. Pour the mixture into a jelly bag (a strainer lined with two to three layers of cheesecloth) and let the juices drip into a bowl. Allow the juices to drip for an hour or two. For clear jelly, do not squeeze the bag or force the jelly through the cheesecloth. Perform a pectin test as described in the Note.

Measure 4 cups of plum juice, adding a little water if necessary. Place in a large pot (at least 4 quarts to allow for bubbling up) and add the sugar. Bring to a boil over medium-high heat and boil to 220°F on a candy thermometer, or until the jelly just sheets from a spoon, forming 2 drops that come together. (For slightly firmer jelly, cook to 222°.)

Skim the foam and preserve according to proper canning methods.

NOTE: *For this recipe, 25 to 50 percent of the plums should be unripe to provide enough tartness (acidity) and pectin to make a jelly. To determine if there is enough pectin in the fruit, after the plum juice has been extracted, combine 2 tablespoons cool plum juice and 2 teaspoons sugar; add 1 tablespoon Epsom salt and stir until all is dissolved. Let the mixture stand for 5 minutes. Then pour the mixture into another bowl. If there is a solid mass of jelly, there is enough pectin for good jelly. Therefore, you will need to use 1 cup sugar per cup of fruit juice. If there are several small masses of jellylike material, then there is moderate pectin, and the jelly will be*

*soft. In this case, use ³⁄₄ cup sugar per cup of juice. If there are many
small masses, there is insufficient pectin, and the addition of commercial pectin will be necessary to make the jelly. Follow the directions included on the pectin package.*

YIELD · 1 QUART

Spiced Pears

Normally, you don't see too many pear trees
on the High Plains. Like apple trees, they're
more common in damper, cooler climates. Both do surprisingly well at the Ranch, though. Watered by flood
irrigation, and protected from gale-force winds by long
windbreakers of Chinese elm and Russian olive trees,
the pear trees bear large, robust fruit. When the pears
ripen in late September, many are preserved in an aromatic, light golden syrup produced from the recipe
below. Unlike Martha Houghton's recipe for peach
syrup, the spices are removed, leaving the syrup almost
clear. These pears are delightful as a simple
stewed dessert or served with vanilla
ice cream.

INGREDIENTS

7 *cups sugar*

2 *cups cider vinegar*

7 *pounds Keaffer or
Bartlett pears,
peeled and cored*

¹⁄₄ *cup whole allspice*

¹⁄₄ *cup whole cloves*

3 *2" pieces of
cinnamon stick*

METHOD

Cut the pears into halves, or quarters if large.

In a pot heat the sugar and vinegar until the sugar is
dissolved. Add the spices tied in a cheesecloth bag. Boil for
10 minutes. Add the prepared fruit and boil until tender;
this may be just a few minutes if the fruit is ripe.

Fill sterilized jars and preserve according to proper canning techniques.

NOTE: *This recipe may be used equally well for peaches.*

YIELD · 4 QUARTS

RELISHES

PEPPER HASH

Healthy doses of brown sugar and cider vinegar give this colorful relish a sweet, tart edge. It's especially appealing on barbecued beef or hamburgers. A dollop of this "hash" atop cream cheese on crackers also makes a pleasing hors d'oeuvre. Unlike pepper jelly, the flavor is mild. So, as a canapé, it offers a nice foil to spicy hors d'oeuvres like pickled okra or nachos.

INGREDIENTS

8 green bell peppers

2 red bell peppers

5 small hot peppers (fresh cayenne or 2 fingerhots)

6 medium onions (3 ounces each)

1½ tablespoons salt

1 cup sugar

2 cups cider vinegar

METHOD

Wash, seed, and devein all the peppers, using rubber gloves when handling the small hot ones. Finely chop the peppers and onions. Place in a bowl, mix together, and pour on boiling water to cover. Let stand for 15 minutes.

Mix the salt, sugar, and vinegar in a large saucepan. Drain the peppers and add to the vinegar mixture. Boil for 15 minutes, cool, and refrigerate, or preserve according to proper canning techniques.

YIELD · 1 ½ QUARTS

SWEET RIPE TOMATO RELISH

Tomatoes, red bell peppers, and cabbage "slaw" pickled bread-and-butter style with turmeric and mustard seed produce an unforgettable relish. Served with smoked ham or liver pâté, it provides an especially piquant contrast to more strongly flavored meats.

INGREDIENTS

4 pounds ripe tomatoes, washed, cored, and diced

½ pound onions, sliced

METHOD

In a large bowl toss the vegetables together with the salt and let stand for 2 hours. Squeeze by handfuls, discarding juices, and place in a pot. Add the remaining ingredients and bring to a boil. Boil for 40 minutes, stirring occasionally. Cool and refrigerate or preserve according to proper canning techniques.

YIELD · 2 QUARTS

- 2 *red bell peppers, washed, seeded, and sliced*
- 1 *pound green cabbage, sliced*
- ¼ *cup salt*
- 1 *cup cider vinegar*
- ¾ *cup sugar*
- ½ *tablespoon ground ginger*
- ½ *tablespoon mustard seed*
- ½ *tablespoon celery seed*
- ¾ *teaspoon ground cinnamon*
- ½ *tablespoon turmeric*
- ⅛ *teaspoon cayenne*

THEO'S CUCUMBER RELISH

The original recipe called for 50 cucumbers. As for Theo, his (or her) identity has unfortunately passed with time. However, this recipe is sure to live on. Twelve cucumbers will produce 3 quarts of thinly sliced pickles that are sweet and sour, yet unusually clean on the palate. As a refrigerated, uncured or "new" pickle, the cucumbers retain their fresh white and bright green colors for a particularly festive look.

METHOD

In a bowl mix the cucumbers, onions, and salt together and let stand an hour or two. Then squeeze out as much liquid as possible and pack into sterilized jars.

In a pot combine the vinegar, sugar, and seasonings, bring to a boil, and boil for a few minutes. Pour over the cucumbers and onions, and preserve according to proper canning techniques.

INGREDIENTS

- 12 *cucumbers, thinly sliced*
- 4 *onions, thinly sliced*
- ¼ *cup salt*
- 2 *cups white vinegar*
- 1 *cup sugar*
- ¼ *teaspoon pepper*
- ¼ *teaspoon ground ginger*
- ½ *teaspoon celery seed*
- ½ *teaspoon mustard seed*

YIELD · 3 QUARTS

THE CHUCK WAGON AT THE HOUGHTON RANCH, ABOUT 1936

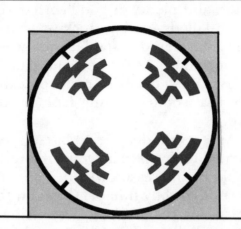

BISCUITS, BREAD, AND ROLLS

W. M. D. Lee and A. E. Reynolds bought out Dolores Duran in 1880 and set up the oasis as "Headquarters." They branded their cattle with the connected letters LE, and before long turned loose several thousand head on unsurveyed land.

In their day, a chuck wagon was dispatched from the Headquarters to trail the cowboys and grazing herds as they roamed many miles from home. The wagon's supplies and equipment were basic, to say the least. Flour, rice, beans, dried fruit, and plenty of good coffee were supplemented by fresh-killed yearling stock or wild game. Potatoes weren't considered a staple; they were too heavy to haul any distance. As for pots and pans, cooks made do with a few Dutch ovens or cast-iron cauldrons and a coffeepot that could be hung from a pot rack over an open fire.

As a result, deep-fried biscuits, or "Cowboy Biscuits," earned their place in western lore. In fact, these sinkers could be the reason why needling the cook is such a big part of cowboy humor. Crisp on the outside and fluffy as cake on the inside, Cowboy Biscuits are doughnutlike cannonballs! While it's clear that chuck wagon cooks took a lot of grief from hungry cowboys, I don't know any stories about cooks who got shot. So, it's a safe bet that if any cowboy carped about his grub, he was too leaden at the end of his meal to get up and do anything about it!

As for Martha Houghton's cooking, when it comes to bread and rolls, her Texas Toast is remembered best—and with no complaints! Cheddar cheese flavored with mustard and Worcestershire is spread on toast, quickly broiled, and then served as finger food at cocktail parties in half slices, or with barbecue.

Among the recipes that follow, some are quite old, having been handed down from one generation to another, such as the recipe for Cornmeal Rolls from Nanny's mother-in-law. Then there's a recipe for Panhandle Brown Bread which no doubt made its way west with an eastern ancestor. Another recipe from a long-gone cook is Lottie's Biscuits. And there is one from Alva T., who is so well-loved for her 7-Up Cake, and in this chapter, her White Corn Bread as well.

BISCUITS

CHEESE BISCUITS

Martha Houghton's buffet parties always included biscuits and they were often made from this clever recipe. It is especially good served with thinly sliced hot smoked tenderloin or baked ham. This recipe calls for sharp Cheddar cheese, but for more pronounced flavor try Gruyère and a pinch or two of cayenne.

METHOD

Preheat the oven to 450°F.

In a bowl sift the flour with the baking powder, mustard, salt, and cayenne, if desired. Add the grated cheese. Cut the shortening in until the mixture resembles coarse meal. Make a well in the center. Pour in the Worcestershire and ⅔ cup milk. Stir quickly with a fork to make a dough just moist enough to form a ball. Add more milk if necessary.

Turn the dough out onto a floured surface and knead briefly. Roll out to ½″ thickness and cut with a floured 2½″ biscuit cutter. Place on an ungreased cookie sheet and bake for 12 to 15 minutes, until lightly golden brown.

YIELD · ABOUT 15 BISCUITS

INGREDIENTS

- 2 cups sifted all-purpose flour
- 1 tablespoon baking powder
- ½ teaspoon dry mustard
- 1 teaspoon salt
  Pinch cayenne (optional)
- 2 ounces grated extra-sharp Cheddar cheese (or Gruyère)
- 5 tablespoons butter or shortening
- 1 teaspoon Worcestershire sauce
- ¾ cup milk

COWBOY BISCUITS

INGREDIENTS

- *1 cup all-purpose flour*
- *2 teaspoons baking powder*
- *½ tablespoon sugar*
- *¼ teaspoon salt*
- *1½ tablespoons butter*
- *1½ tablespoons solid vegetable shortening*
- *⅓ cup milk*
- *Vegetable oil for frying*

These deep-fried "beauties" are chuck-wagon classics. Without ovens, the only way trail cooks could make biscuits was to fry them in kettles called "Dutch ovens." The result was hearty and heavy, but in its own way, delicious.

Split them in half and ladle some Cream Gravy over a piece or two with your Fried Chicken for "Chicken and Biscuits." Or, if you want to test their resiliency, try half a biscuit with some of Gar's Chili Salsa. It's a tasty way to find out that these Cowboy Biscuits can stand up to anything!

METHOD

In a bowl sift the flour with the baking powder, sugar, and salt. Cut in the butter and shortening until the mixture resembles coarse meal. Stir the milk into the mixture with a fork, using just enough milk to make a soft dough.

Turn the dough out onto a well-floured board and knead gently for half a minute. Either divide the dough into 8 portions, roll into balls, and flatten to ½" thickness, or roll out to ½" thickness and cut into biscuits with a 2" or 2½" biscuit cutter.

Heat 1" of oil in a large heavy skillet. Drop the biscuits into the hot oil and fry for 4 to 5 minutes, turning once halfway through the cooking time. Do not crowd the biscuits in the pan. Drain on paper towels and serve hot.

YIELD · ABOUT 8 BISCUITS

LOTTIE'S BISCUITS

This recipe for baking powder biscuits was a real find among Nanny's collection. Not too fluffy and relatively "short," Lottie's dough is just great for cobbler topping, fried biscuits, strawberry short-cake, or, of course, good old biscuits—especially served hot with butter and homemade jam.

METHOD

Preheat the oven to 450°F.

In a bowl sift the flour with the baking powder, sugar, and salt. Cut in the butter and shortening until the mixture resembles coarse meal. Stir the milk into the mixture with a fork, using just enough milk to make a soft dough.

Turn the dough out onto a floured board and knead gently for 30 seconds. Roll the dough out to ½″ thickness and cut with a 2½″ biscuit cutter. Place on an ungreased cookie sheet and bake for 10 to 15 minutes, until a light butterscotch color.

YIELD · ABOUT 30 BISCUITS

INGREDIENTS

4 cups sifted all-purpose flour

8 teaspoons baking powder

2 tablespoons sugar

1½ teaspoons salt

6 tablespoons butter

6 tablespoons solid vegetable shortening

1½ cups milk

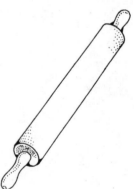

BREAD

PANHANDLE BROWN BREAD

Winter at the Ranch can be cold and intense. Temperatures drop to zero quickly and stay there. The wind howls along the High Plains endlessly and, for three months, the range is bleak and severe. Strong coffee or tea with something sweet and hot, like toasted brown bread with butter, was often served to warm up cowboys who came in cold and raw after a long day in the saddle.

How Boston brown bread made its way to the Panhandle is anybody's guess. There's no question that they make it a little differently in the Panhandle, though. The cornmeal is more coarse, and less baking soda makes the bread denser. First steamed in a bowl, the bread is then unmolded and baked. As cake, it's too dry and hard, but there's nothing quite like a rich slice toasted with butter and served on a cold winter's day.

INGREDIENTS

- *1 cup coarse yellow cornmeal*
- *1 cup all-purpose flour*
- *2 cups whole-wheat flour*
- *1 cup raisins*
- *1 tablespoon salt*
- *2 cups molasses*
- *1 cup sour milk or buttermilk*
- *1 cup milk*
- *1 tablespoon baking soda dissolved in 1 tablespoon hot water*

METHOD

Generously butter three 1-quart pudding molds, plus three "rounds" of aluminum foil.

Place the cornmeal, flours, raisins, and salt in a mixing bowl. Add the molasses, milk, and dissolved baking soda. Stir to mix thoroughly. Fill the pudding molds three-quarters full. Cover each with the foil and tie the foil in place.

Fill a kettle with a rack with 1″ of water; bring to a boil. Place the molds on the rack and steam, covered, for 3 hours; replenish the boiling water as necessary. Unmold immediately, and bake on a rack for 20 minutes at 350°F. Let the loaves cool and serve immediately, or warm before serving.

YIELD · 3 LOAVES

SPOON BREAD

As spoon breads go, this one's long on corn flavor and is almost like a soufflé. For a more traditional, puddinglike texture, allow less baking time.

METHOD

Preheat the oven to 350°F. Grease a 2-quart baking dish.

In a saucepan stir the cornmeal into 2 cups milk and bring to a boil. Beat the egg yolks. Then add the rest of the milk, the egg yolks, butter, baking powder, and salt and mix well.

Beat the egg whites until they form stiff peaks, but are not dry, and gently fold into the mixture.

Pour the batter into the baking dish and bake for 30 to 35 minutes, until it's slightly brown and crusty on top. Serve with a spoon, as bread should not be quite firm.

YIELD · 8 SERVINGS

INGREDIENTS

- *1 cup coarse yellow cornmeal*
- *3 cups milk*
- *3 eggs, separated*
- *2 tablespoons butter*
- *3/4 teaspoon baking powder*
- *3/4 teaspoon salt*

TEXAS TOAST

This was one of Martha Houghton's most popular finger foods. Copies of this simple hors d'oeuvre popped up throughout her extensive collection of recipes. She must have taught it to many, many cooks because instructions were written out on anything that was handy—the backs of envelopes, obsolete stationery, sales receipts, and shopping lists. They all provided the same toasty treat, sharp Cheddar spurred on by dry mustard.

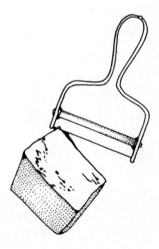

INGREDIENTS

- 4 ounces sharp Cheddar cheese, shredded
- 1 stick (¹/₂ cup) of butter or margarine
- ¹/₈ teaspoon pepper
- 1 teaspoon dry mustard
- 16 thick slices of bread

METHOD

Preheat the oven to 400°F.

Combine the cheese, butter or margarine, pepper and mustard in the top of a double boiler or in a heavy-bottomed saucepan. Heat until blended and smooth, stirring with a wire whisk.

Meanwhile, toast the slices of bread.

Spread the cheese mixture on the toasted bread, cut into quarters, and bake until browned, about 5 minutes.

NOTE: *Two or 3 drops of Worcestershire sauce on each quarter toast will enhance the sharp "cheesy," flavor of this hors d'oeuvre.*

YIELD · ABOUT 64 SQUARES

WHITE CORN BREAD

 Alva T. recalled that "Mrs. Houghton liked her corn bread thin and white, crumbly with just a touch of sugar." This is it. Nanny had it served most often with fish, but it's nice with chicken or pork.

INGREDIENTS

- 1 cup white cornmeal
- 1 teaspoon salt
- 1 tablespoon sugar
- ¹/₄ teaspoon baking soda
- 1¹/₂ teaspoons baking powder
- 1 egg, well beaten
- ³/₄ cup buttermilk

METHOD

Preheat the oven to 425°F. Preheat a 9″ cast-iron frying pan in the oven.

In a bowl sift the cornmeal, salt, sugar, baking soda, and baking powder together. Add the egg and buttermilk and beat well.

Remove the hot pan from the oven, grease quickly, and pour the batter into it. Place back in the oven and bake for 15 minutes, or until brown and a knife inserted in the center comes out clean.

Invert the frying pan over a rack or cutting board and turn out the bread. Serve browned side up.

YIELD · 8 SERVINGS

ROLLS

CORNMEAL ROLLS

With the closest grocery some 40 miles from the Ranch, a sudden shortage of ingredients could lead to ingenious substitutions and new recipes. In this case, "stretching" flour with coarse-ground cornmeal added a new dimension to this simple recipe for Parker House rolls. The cornmeal adds a wonderful nutty flavor and a texture akin to whole wheat.

METHOD

Preheat the oven to 450°F.

In a bowl sift the dry ingredients. Cut in the shortening. Beat the egg slightly with the milk and add to the dry ingredients.

Toss on a floured board; knead slightly. Roll ½″ thick and cut with a large (3″) biscuit cutter. With the back of a knife, make a crease just off center on each round. Brush with butter, and fold the smaller part over, like Parker House rolls. Press the fold gently. Bake in the hot oven for 12 to 15 minutes.

Serve hot.

YIELD · ABOUT 8 ROLLS

INGREDIENTS

1½ cups all-purpose flour

¾ cup coarse cornmeal

4 teaspoons baking powder

1 teaspoon salt

¼ teaspoon baking soda

4 tablespoons solid vegetable shortening

1 egg

¾ cup buttermilk

ICEBOX ROLLS

INGREDIENTS

2 *cups milk, or 1*
cup milk plus 1
cup water

½ *cup solid vegetable*
shortening

½ *cup sugar*

1 *package yeast*

4½ *cups all-purpose*
flour

½ *tablespoon salt*

½ *teaspoon baking*
soda

½ *teaspoon baking*
powder, rounded

To Martha Houghton, convenience food was something that could be made in advance and used as needed. These Icebox Rolls are a good example: With the dough made, you merely roll and cut what you need, let it rise for 2 hours, and bake for 12 to 15 minutes. The dough keeps for at least 5 days. Once baked, the rolls reheat nicely when wrapped in foil and baked at 350°F until soft. As rolls go, these are slightly sweet and finely textured. Baked in the Parker House style, they're an elegant complement to roasted fowl or meats.

METHOD

Place the milk, shortening, and sugar in a saucepan; bring to a boil. Cool to lukewarm and dissolve the yeast in the mixture.

Sift in 2½ cups flour and mix well. Let the dough rise for 2 hours. Add the salt, baking soda, baking powder, and remaining flour, and knead, adding a little more flour if necessary until smooth and no longer sticky. Place in a buttered bowl, cover with plastic wrap, weight down with a plate and two to three 1-pound cans, and place in the refrigerator. The dough will keep up to 5 days.

Cut the amount of dough needed about 2 hours before time to bake. Roll the dough out to ⅓" thickness and cut with a 3" cookie or biscuit cutter. Brush with melted butter and make an indentation across the center of the round. Fold one edge over, but not even with the bottom edge—in other words, the edges should not quite meet. Let rise until doubled. Bake in a preheated 400°F oven for 12 to 15 minutes.

YIELD · ABOUT 24 ROLLS

MASHED POTATO ROLLS

Nanny never wasted anything. The amount of mashed potatoes called for is seemingly small, but its effect is not. Without it, these rolls are just good old, light and feathery icebox rolls made with eggs. The potatoes, though, add weight and crustiness, making the rolls more coarse and chewy.

INGREDIENTS

2 *cups milk*

2 *tablespoons butter*

1 *cup cooked mashed potatoes*

1 *package yeast dissolved in* ½ *cup warm water*

½ *cup sugar*

1 *egg, well beaten*

1 *tablespoon salt*

7–8 *cups all-purpose flour*

METHOD

In a saucepan scald the milk. Add the butter and let melt. When lukewarm, add the potatoes and dissolved yeast. Add the sugar, egg, and salt; mix well.

Place 7 cups flour in a large bowl. Stir in the milk mixture and combine until smooth. Add more flour as necessary to make a stiff but smooth dough.

Place in a greased bowl, cover with plastic wrap, and place in the refrigerator. Use any time after 24 hours, but within 5 days.

About 2 hours before serving, remove the desired amount of dough from the refrigerator. Roll out to ⅓″ thick, cut with a 3″ biscuit cutter, shape into Parker House rolls (see page 75), and let rise until doubled. Bake in a preheated 425°F oven for 12 to 15 minutes, or until well browned.

YIELD · ABOUT 36 ROLLS

ORANGE ROLLS

INGREDIENTS

- 2 *oranges*
- 1 *package yeast dissolved in ½ cup warm water*
- 1 *egg, beaten*
- 1 *tablespoon butter, melted*
- 1 *tablespoon sugar*
- 1 *teaspoon salt*
- 3 *cups all-purpose flour*

ICING

- 1 *orange*
- 1½ *cups powdered sugar*
- 1 *tablespoon butter, room temperature*

Just the thought of these sweet rolls makes me taste oranges. Whenever these rolls were made, the air in the kitchen would be filled with the steamy aroma of freshly baked bread and the essence of orange. Walking into the kitchen on early mornings and getting a heady whiff was a great way to wake up. Needless to say, when they were served at the Ranch, orders for more sausage and eggs went down as quickly as requests for more orange rolls went up!

This recipe is adapted from the 1928 *Woman's Club of Fort Worth Cookbook.*

METHOD

Remove the zest from the oranges, grate, and save. Squeeze the oranges and save the juice and pulp, removing the seeds from the pulp.

In a bowl combine the dissolved yeast, egg, butter, sugar, salt, zest, juice, and pulp. Add the flour and beat until smooth, adding more flour if necessary to make a manageable dough. Place the dough in a buttered bowl, cover, and let rise until doubled in bulk, about an hour.

Preheat the oven to 400°F.

Knead and shape the rolls. To make cloverleaf rolls, divide the dough evenly into 45 to 54 pieces. Gently roll each piece into a ball. Place three pieces in each 2½" cup of a greased muffin tin. To make plain rolls, divide the dough evenly into 15 to 18 balls and place each in the 2½" cups of a greased muffin tin. Let rise again until doubled, about an hour. Bake for 12 to 15 minutes or until light golden brown.

While the rolls are baking, make the icing. Remove the zest from the orange and mince. Squeeze the orange into a bowl. Combine the sugar, butter, zest, and enough juice to make a stiff icing.

Spread the rolls with icing immediately upon removal from the oven.

YIELD · 15–18 ROLLS

MUFFINS AND SUCH

BRAN GEMS

Breakfast at the Ranch just wasn't served without something baked or toasted. Nanny's bran muffins were toasted "gems," which could just as easily have been called "diamonds," as in diamonds in the rough. This recipe is adapted from *The Five O'Clock Tea Club Cookbook,* published in Fort Worth as a fundraiser in the 1920s. These muffins are solid and coarse, almost inedible as is. Toasted with butter, though, they soften up and come to life with a sweet, nutty bran flavor.

METHOD

Preheat the oven to 350°F. Butter a muffin pan or two.

In a bowl mix the dry ingredients together.

In another bowl beat the egg and milk together. Stir in half the bran mixture. Mix well, add the butter, then the rest of the bran mixture. Stir just until mixed. Fill the muffin tins half full. Bake for 20 to 30 minutes, or until slightly rounded on top and a little crusty.

YIELD · 12 MUFFINS

INGREDIENTS

- 1 cup bran
- 1 cup whole-wheat flour
- 1 teaspoon salt
- 1 tablespoon sugar
- 1 tablespoon baking powder
- 1 egg
- 7/8 cup milk
- 3 tablespoons butter, melted

CHEESE WAFERS

Hot hors d'ouevres served around the Christmas holidays invariably included these cheesy little nuggets. Made from "short" piecrust dough (the easiest to make), they can be made ahead and reheated just before serving.

INGREDIENTS

- *1 cup sifted all-purpose flour*
- *1/4 cup butter or margarine*
- *1/4 pound Cheddar cheese, grated*
- *1/4 teaspoon salt*
- *2 tablespoons cold water*
- *1/8 teaspoon cayenne*

METHOD

Preheat the oven to 375°F. Grease a baking sheet.

Place the flour in a bowl or the workbowl of a food processor. Add the butter or margarine and cut in until well blended. Mix in the cheese and salt. Mix in the water and cayenne thoroughly.

Press the mixture into a mass. Form into a log 1¾" in diameter and slice ⅛" as if for cookies. Place on the baking sheet and bake for 10 to 15 minutes, until golden brown. Serve hot, or reheat before serving. For a festive touch, top with pecan halves before baking.

YIELD · 18–20 PUFFS

JALAPEÑO CORN STICKS

Jalapeños added to corn muffins or bread is a fine example of how South met West at the Houghton Ranch. If you don't have a corn-stick mold, the batter bakes just fine in a muffin tin, cake pan, or even a black cast-iron frying pan!

INGREDIENTS

- *¾ cup all-purpose flour*
- *1½ cups yellow cornmeal*
- *2 tablespoons sugar*
- *1 teaspoon salt (continued)*

METHOD

Preheat the oven to 425°F. Grease a corn-stick mold or 3-inch muffin tins.

In a bowl stir together the flour, cornmeal, sugar, salt, and baking powder. Stir in the eggs, butter, and jalapeño peppers. Add the baking soda and then stir in the buttermilk; mix thoroughly. Pour into the prepared mold or tins and bake for 15 to 20 minutes, or until golden.

1 tablespoon baking powder

2 eggs, beaten

3 tablespoons butter, melted

2 fresh jalapeño peppers, seeded, deveined, and minced (2 tablespoons)

1/2 teaspoon baking soda

1 1/2 cups warmed buttermilk

YIELD · 12 CORN STICKS OR MUFFINS

HUSH PUPPIES

In the South, Hush Puppies are served along with fried perch or catfish like bacon with eggs. Martha Houghton's recipe produces little fried corn balls the size of golf balls. Fried crisp and dark brown on the outside, they're moister on the inside than most.

To some, Hush Puppies are an acquired taste. However, once you get used to the taste of corn and onion with deep-fried fish, you might just "bark" for more.

INGREDIENTS

Vegetable oil or lard for frying

2 cups fine-ground cornmeal

1 tablespoon flour

1 teaspoon baking soda

1 tablespoon salt

6 tablespoons chopped onion

1 egg

1−1 1/4 cups buttermilk

METHOD

Preheat the oil to 375°F.

In a bowl mix the dry ingredients together. Add the onion, egg, and 1 cup buttermilk. Stir to blend. If the mixture seems too dry, add more of the buttermilk, but take care; the batter must be firm enough to hold together when fried—if it is too soupy, you will have fried crumbs.

Drop the batter by the tablespoonful into the hot oil and fry until dark brown, turning once. Fry the hush puppies in batches, without crowding, and reheat the oil to 375° between batches. Drain on paper towels and serve hot.

NOTE: *The coarser the meal, the less liquid you need to bind.*

YIELD · ABOUT 48 HUSH PUPPIES

NANNY'S DAUGHTER, MARTHA HOUGHTON GARNER (*FAR RIGHT*), WITH CHAMPION HEREFORD BULL, 1947

MEAT, FOWL, AND FISH

The first cattle to roam the Houghton Ranch were Missouri Durhams. By 1881, the herd was expanded through purchases and breeding to twenty thousand head. Early on, the rangey longhorns were bred to beefier breeds. Then, as cattle drives gave way to shipping by rail, the longhorns were phased out altogether; there was literally no room for their antlerlike horns in railroad cars designed to hold twenty-six head cheek by jowl.

By the time Ted Houghton took over the management of the Ranch,

Herefords were the most favored breed in the Panhandle. He was quite committed to building a purebred herd, and at his death in 1957, was widely recognized for having accomplished his goal on a grand scale.

In the 1960s crossbreeding became popular all over again, and Herefords were crossbred with Angus, Charolois, Brahman, and other more exotic strains to produce faster maturing, heartier animals. Now, almost thirty years later, Ted Houghton's great nephews Malcolm and Jim Shelton graze cattle specially bred to thrive at the Ranch to meet the demand for top-quality choice, lean beef.

Not surprisingly, beef was popular at Nanny's table— as a topic of discussion as well as on the plate. And, of course, it was prepared every way typical of the South and West—barbecued, rendered into chili, chicken fried, broiled, grilled, roasted, or turned into Nanny's "smothered roast"—all seasoned in her inimitable peppery fashion. More recipes for beef follow in the chapter on barbecue.

However, as the following recipes show, Nanny served far more than beef. Porkers and chickens raised right at the Ranch and even fresh fish from the lakes (and not too distant streams of Colorado) were served for tasty variety.

BEEF

LIVER AND ONIONS

Nanny's recipe for liver and onions is simple and fast. Thinly sliced liver and butter mixed with a little oil allow for quick cooking before the butter burns and loses its sweetness. The onions, cooked soft but not mushy, provide a sweet, slightly sharp contrast that makes this often underappreciated dish taste "just right."

METHOD

Heat 1 tablespoon butter and 1 tablespoon oil in a heavy skillet and sauté the onion rings and garlic until golden. Remove from the pan and keep warm. Wipe out the skillet.

Add another tablespoon each of butter and oil to the skillet and heat over high heat. Dredge the liver slices lightly in flour and sauté in the hot butter and oil for 1 to 2 minutes per side, turning once. (Slices ¼" thick will take just 1 minute each side, ½" thick closer to 2 minutes per side.) The liver should be pink inside. Remove when done and keep warm while repeating with remaining slices, adding more butter and oil as necessary, and regulating heat as necessary.

Arrange the liver on a hot platter, sprinkle with salt and pepper, top with the onions and optional garlic, and serve immediately.

NOTE: *If you do not want to serve the garlic with the onions, just quarter the clove.*

INGREDIENTS

- 4 tablespoons butter
- 4 tablespoons vegetable oil
- 2 onions, sliced and separated into rings
- 1 garlic clove, minced (see note)
- 1½ pounds calf's or beef liver, thinly sliced
- ½ cup all-purpose flour

  Salt and pepper to taste

YIELD · 4 SERVINGS

RANCH FRIED STEAK

INGREDIENTS

All-purpose flour
Vegetable oil for frying
Salt and pepper
4 *pounds round steak cut into ½"-thick slices*

Martha Houghton's approach to the Texas classic, chicken fried steak, features three different methods. First, the steaks are seasoned before they are tenderized; second, the steaks are not dipped in egg or batter but merely dredged in flour; and finally, they are gently steamed after cooking. The result is juicy, flavorful meat with a tender crust. Indeed, the steak is so moist, its typical sidekick, cream gravy, is rarely served at the Ranch.

M E T H O D

Generously salt and pepper a slice of steak, using ½ teaspoon salt and pepper on each side. With the back of the blade of a heavy knife or cleaver, vigorously pound the steak, pounding the seasonings into the meat to tenderize. The steak should be well crosshatched, like cubed steak. Repeat on the other side of the meat; continue with the remaining slices. Cut each steak into halves or thirds. Dredge the slices in flour.

Pour ¼" of oil into a heavy skillet and heat until it bubbles when the tip of a steak is lowered into it. Fry the steak slices until dark brown on one side (3–5 minutes); turn and fry until dark brown on the second side. As the steak is cooked, remove it to a rack in a steamer or a Dutch oven containing ½" of simmering water. Make sure the rack does not touch the water. Continue to fry the steak, adding more oil to the pan as necessary and always reheating to hot before adding more meat. When all the steaks are cooked, remove from the steamer and serve immediately.

YIELD · 8 SERVINGS

SHORT RIBS

A short rib dinner at the Ranch was always a treat. It was one of Martha Houghton's favorites and she served it with great pleasure. Mounds of ribs would be brought to the table on hot platters accompanied by lots of barbecue sauce. Fresh corn on the cob, green beans with ham hocks, and sliced tomatoes and Spanish onions turned this midday meal into a veritable feast. Somehow, though, we always found room for some pineapple sherbet and a piece of Alva T.'s toasted 7-Up Cake.

Nanny didn't care too much for gravy and, as a result, rarely served it. However, I have included an onion pan gravy here because it's so good with these ribs.

INGREDIENTS

8 pounds short ribs
Salt and pepper

ONION PAN GRAVY

2 tablespoons
  drippings
½ cup chopped onion
2 tablespoons flour
2 cups milk
  cup chopped onion
2 tablespoons flour
2 cups milk

METHOD

Preheat the oven to 450°F.

Place the ribs on a rack in a roasting pan and sprinkle with salt and pepper. Bake for 20 minutes, then turn the oven down to 350° and bake for 2 hours more.

Remove the ribs and keep warm. Remove the rack from the roasting pan and pour off all but 2 tablespoons of fat from the pan. Scrape loose as much of the drippings as possible and pour them with the remaining fat into a cast-iron skillet. Add the onion to the skillet and sauté over medium heat to a deep brown. Stir in the flour until smooth and slowly stir in the milk. Bring to a simmer, stirring, and simmer for 5 minutes. Correct the seasoning and serve hot with the ribs.

YIELD · 4–6 SERVINGS

SMOTHERED ROUND STEAK

INGREDIENTS

2 *slices of salt pork (3 ounces)*

1 *medium onion, chopped*

2 *pounds round steak*

1½ *cups water*

1 *teaspoon salt*

1 *teaspoon black pepper*

1½ *tablespoons butter*

2 *tablespoons flour*

⅛ *teaspoon red pepper flakes (optional)*

 Martha Houghton earned a tender place in the hearts of many with this easy recipe for a cut of meat that is typically tough.

METHOD

Fry out the salt pork, remove, and discard. Add the chopped onion to the fat and sauté until brown. Remove and reserve the onion. Place the steak in the pan and sear on both sides. Pour the water over the steak, add the salt and pepper, and bring to a boil. Cover, lower heat, and simmer for an hour, or until tender, turning once after 30 minutes.

Remove the steak and stock and set aside. Add the butter to the pan and, when melted, add the flour; stir to blend. Return the stock and onions to the pan, and bring to a boil, stirring constantly. Add the red pepper flakes, if desired, and correct the seasoning.

Pour the gravy over the steak and serve.

YIELD · 4 SERVINGS

PORK

GLAZED HAM

Served hot, this glazed ham is really very good, but cold and sliced thin, it's a feast. Presented with Nanny's Mustard Pickles and either of her potato salads this makes a classic, simple Sunday supper.

INGREDIENTS

1	ham with bone
25–50	whole cloves
³⁄₄–1	cup spicy brown mustard
2	cups apple cider
½	cup plum or grape jelly

METHOD

Preheat the oven to 325°F.

Trim the ham fat to within ¼″ to ½″ of the meat. Score the fat in a diamond-shape pattern, place a clove at each intersection, poke it into the meat with the handle of a small wooden spoon, and paint the ham with some of the mustard, reserving ½ cup for the glaze.

Place the ham on a rack in a roasting pan. Pour the cider into the pan. Bake the ham for 25 minutes per pound for small hams or 20 minutes per pound for large or whole hams, or until the internal temperature registers 160°F on a meat thermometer. Baste occasionally with the cider. About 30 minutes before the ham is done, mix the remaining mustard with the jelly and brush on the ham to glaze. Brush any remaining glaze on 15 minutes later.

Serve hot or warm.

YIELD · ALLOW ½ POUND OF UNCOOKED HAM PER PERSON.

SAUSAGE

2½ pounds pork (not too fat)

⅛ teaspoon cayenne

1 tablespoon salt

2 teaspoons ground sage

½ tablespoon black pepper

1 tablespoon brown sugar

In its original form, this recipe called for enough ingredients to make 100 pounds of well-seasoned sausage. Every year, just before Christmas, hogs would be slaughtered and then great batches of sausage were put up in 1-pound bags as Christmas gifts from the Ranch for appreciative family and friends. Of course, this recipe has been adjusted for convenience. The flavor, though, tastes like it just came from the Houghton Ranch.

METHOD

Cut the pork into pieces for grinding. Mix the remaining ingredients together in a bowl and sprinkle over the pork pieces. Toss to mix well. Grind the pork in a meat grinder.

Shape the pork into ¼-pound patties each ½″ thick, and fry over medium heat, starting the patties in a cold frying pan, and cooking about 10 minutes a side, or until the juices run clear. Serve hot.

YIELD · 10 PATTIES

SMOTHERED PORK CHOPS

What I remember best about these chops is not the spicy gravy or the tender meat that would fall off the bone. Instead, I recall a hilarious dinner when Martha Bivins, then age 12, turned to Nanny and wanted to know if we were eating the pigs she helped feed—Henry and Henrietta. Nanny sidestepped the question by explaining that the chops came from pigs raised the year before. "But, Nanny," Martha insisted, "they were Henry and Henrietta, too." "Well, don't tell their replacements," Nanny quipped as she avoided the sticky question, "and they won't catch on!"

M E T H O D

Heat the vegetable shortening in a 10″ frying pan until hot.

Salt and pepper the chops to taste. Dredge in the ½ cup flour. Fry the chops until butterscotch brown on both sides (about 5–6 minutes per side). Push chops around a bit to avoid sticking. Remove the chops from the pan, lower heat, and fry the onion rings until limp. Remove the onions.

Drain the oil from the pan. Deglaze the pan with the water, stirring to dissolve all bits. Pour off the liquid and save. Melt the butter in the pan and stir in the 2 tablespoons flour until smooth. Add the milk gradually, stirring until smooth. Then add the deglazing liquid, and heat the gravy to a simmer, stirring constantly. Return the chops, onions, and any juices that have accumulated to the pan. Baste the chops well with the gravy. Cover and simmer over low heat for an hour, or until the chops are tender.

Y I E L D · 2 S E R V I N G S

INGREDIENTS

½ cup solid vegetable shortening
Salt and pepper
4 ½″ thick pork chops
½ cup all-purpose flour, plus 2 tablespoons
1 medium onion, sliced and separated into rings
¼ cup water
2 tablespoons butter
⅔ cup milk

ONE OF THE

"HENRIETTAS"—

AND SOME FUTURE

HENRIETTAS

INGREDIENTS

3 cups cooked
  chicken meat (¾
  pound)

½ small onion,
  minced

3 eggs, hard-
  cooked, minced

9 saltines, mashed
  into crumbs

½ teaspoon celery
  seed

½ teaspoon ground
  cloves

½ teaspoon salt

½ teaspoon pepper

½–1 cup chicken
  stock

8–10 whole cloves
  (optional)

2 eggs, beaten
  Cracker meal
  Vegetable oil for
  frying

CHICKEN

CHICKEN CROQUETTES

No leftover chicken ever had it so good. This recipe for croquettes, from Nanny's dog-eared copy of *The Woman's Club of Fort Worth Cookbook*, is basic and to the point. It's just chicken, stock, hard-cooked eggs, and a touch of onion with a wonderful aroma imparted by whole cloves. These croquettes are firmer than most and their mild flavor is easily enhanced by a pat of butter when the croquettes are split in half before eating. That's a good time to fish out the whole clove because it's one surprise that might be unpleasant to bite.

METHOD

Using a meat grinder or food processor, chop the chicken finely.

In a bowl combine the chicken with the onion, egg, and cracker crumbs. Add the seasonings. Stir in enough of the chicken stock to barely hold the mixture together. Form into 2″ haystacks, logs, or patties. (If the mixture gets too wet, it won't hold a shape.) Stick a clove in the top of each haystack, if desired. Dip the croquettes in the beaten egg and roll in the cracker meal. Heat the oil to 375°F. Fry 3 or 4 minutes to golden brown in the hot oil.

Drain on paper towels and serve hot.

YIELD · 8–10 CROQUETTES

CHICKEN IN DRESSING

This simple Sunday dinner was a hit when Lillie introduced it to us at the Ranch. Boneless chicken breasts topped with a tasty stuffing are baked, covered, and then browned for a crispy coating during the last 15 or 20 minutes. Nanny was as fond of this dish for its clever simplicity as she was for its pleasant flavor.

METHOD

Preheat the oven to 350°F. Butter a baking dish.

Place the chicken breasts in the baking dish. In a bowl mix the rest of the ingredients together and spread over the chicken. Cover the dish and bake for 45 minutes. Remove the cover and bake for 15 to 20 minutes longer. Serve immediately. This dish may be run under a hot broiler to brown, if desired.

YIELD · 4 SERVINGS

INGREDIENTS

- 2 boneless chicken breasts, halved
- 2 cups slightly stale bread cubes or stuffing
- 1/4 cup chopped onion
- 1/4 cup chopped celery
- 1/2 teaspoon salt
- 1/4 teaspoon pepper
- 1/4 teaspoon paprika
- 2 tablespoons chopped fresh parsley
- 3/4 cup chicken broth

FRIED CHICKEN

INGREDIENTS

2½–3 *pounds chicken*

1 *cup milk*

1 *cup heavy cream*

Vegetable oil for frying

2½ *teaspoons salt*

1½ *teaspoons pepper*

1¼ *cups all-purpose flour, plus 2 tablespoons*

½ *teaspoon paprika*

1 *egg*

½ *cup chicken broth*

I could wax poetic about the fried chicken served at the Ranch, but I'll just say that this is happy food. Just the thought of Nanny's Fried Chicken makes me smile. For "Chicken and Biscuits," serve these with deep-fried Cowboy Biscuits and Cream Gravy.

METHOD

Rinse the chicken and cut into 10 pieces: drumsticks, thighs, wings, and breasts, each cut into 2 pieces. Mix the milk and cream together in a bowl and soak the chicken pieces in the mixture for at least 2 hours at room temperature.

Pour the oil 1″ deep into a Dutch oven or deep heavy skillet with a lid. Heat the oil to hot, but not smoking (375°F).

Remove the chicken pieces from the milk mixture and pat dry. Save the milk mixture. Mix the salt and pepper together and sprinkle half the mixture evenly over the chicken. Mix the remaining salt-pepper mixture with the 1¼ cups of flour and the paprika. Beat the egg with ½ cup of the milk-cream mixture.

Dredge the chicken in the flour, shake off the excess and dip each piece in the egg mixture, coating thoroughly. Dredge again in the flour, and shake off the excess. Place the chicken pieces, skin side down, in the hot oil, cover the pan, and fry, allowing 12 to 13 minutes for dark meat pieces, 8 minutes for white meat, turning once halfway through cooking time. The juices should run clear when the meat is pierced, and the chicken should be a dark butterscotch color. Drain the chicken on paper towels and keep warm in a barely warm oven.

Pour off all but 1 tablespoon of the oil from the pan. Add the 2 tablespoons flour, stir to mix thoroughly and to loosen any bits in the pan, and brown lightly. Stir in the remaining milk and cream mixture and the chicken broth, and bring to a simmer, stirring. Simmer for 3 to 5 minutes, correct the seasoning, and serve hot with the chicken.

NOTE: *If frying biscuits (see Cowboy Biscuits, page 70), return the oil to 375°F after removing the chicken and fry the biscuits for 4 to 5 minutes, turning once. Drain on paper towels.*

YIELD · 4 SERVINGS

PRESSED CHICKEN

Another one of Martha Houghton's party dishes, this attractive mold is quite nice for summer entertaining and conveniently serves 8 to 12 people. The old-fashioned relish mentioned in this recipe, chowchow, adds piquant contrast to the chicken and mayonnaise. For variety, though, try replacing the chowchow with curry and chutney.

METHOD

Lightly oil a 4- to 6-cup decorative or ring mold.

Soften the gelatin in the chicken broth, then heat the mixture in a saucepan until the gelatin is dissolved. Let the mixture cool until it just starts to set. Stir in the mayonnaise until thoroughly combined. Stir in the remaining ingredients, except the lettuce, seasoning highly with salt and pepper. Mix well and pack into the mold. Chill until firm, at least 6 hours.

Unmold onto a bed of lettuce and serve in slices.

VARIATION: *Omit the chowchow, and add 1 to 2 tablespoons curry powder to the mayonnaise before blending it with the chicken broth mixture and ¼ cup chopped chutney with the other ingredients.*

YIELD · 8–12 SERVINGS

INGREDIENTS

1½ envelopes of
   unflavored gelatin
1½ cups chicken broth
  1 cup mayonnaise
  2 cups cooked
    chicken, cut into
    ½" dice
  1 cup celery, cut into
    ½" dice
½ cup lightly
    browned slivered
    almonds
  3 eggs, hard-cooked,
    diced
  1 tablespoon capers
¼ cup chopped
    chowchow
    Salt and pepper
    Lettuce leaves

INGREDIENTS

*Fillets from 1
2–3-pound
freshwater bass*

1 *cup olive oil*

Juice of 1 lemon

1/2 *teaspoon salt*

1/4 *teaspoon pepper*

1/4 *teaspoon dried
tarragon (optional)*

1/4 *cup unseasoned
bread crumbs
(optional)*

F I S H

BROILED BASS

Bass fishing in the lakes at the Ranch is nothing short of terrific. Ted Houghton loved to pull real "lunkers" out of these waters, and his descendants and friends are still landing them as he did more than 30 years ago. For all its simplicity, this recipe turns out fish with a light crust that's moist, flaky, and not too "fishy." It's an ideal recipe for any kind of fish suitable for broiling, such as halibut or red snapper.

M E T H O D

In a pan marinate the fillets in the oil, lemon juice, salt, pepper, and tarragon for 2 hours, refrigerated.

Preheat the broiler. Grease a baking pan.

Remove the fillets from the marinade and place on the pan, skin side down. Sprinkle with the bread crumbs, if desired. Broil the fish until the flesh is opaque and flaky, about 10 minutes per measured inch of thickness of the fillets. Watch carefully so that the fish does not overcook and dry out. If bread crumbs are used, they should be just medium brown.

Serve immediately.

YIELD · 2–3 SERVINGS

FRIED CATFISH

Among the many hands at the Ranch fishing in one of the six lakes is a favorite pastime. On a hot summer evening or afternoon off, it's a great way to catch the breezes that blow across the water, and to have some fun. Every summer a friendly rivalry develops to see who can catch the greatest "trophy" and, inevitably, some enterprising "sportsman" sets out a trotline, which is the way most catfish are taken. These evil-looking fish put up a fight equal to any bass and make an equally exciting dinner.

The recipe below turns out crisp, golden fillets without an egg dip or batter. However, this mild, dense fish can be quite dry, so be careful not to overcook it. Since your fillets will vary in thickness, frying time should vary accordingly. The estimated time of 3 to 4 minutes for ½"-thick fillets is indicated as a benchmark. Dipping the catfish in a beaten egg and dredging the fillets in cornmeal can enhance your chances of moist fish, but the result will not be as crisp or attractive. Personally, I like the simpler approach.

INGREDIENTS

Vegetable oil for frying

2 pounds ½"-thick catfish fillets

1 cup yellow cornmeal

1 teaspoon salt

¾ teaspoon pepper

⅛ teaspoon garlic powder, or to taste

METHOD

Pour the oil 2" deep into a high-sided skillet and preheat to 375°F.

Rinse the fillets in cold water and pat dry. Mix the cornmeal, salt, pepper, and garlic powder thoroughly. Dredge the fillets in the cornmeal and fry, a few at a time, until golden brown, 3 to 4 minutes. Drain on paper towels. Reheat the oil to 375° between batches. Serve the fish hot.

SERVING SUGGESTION: *It's traditional and delicious to serve the catfish with Hush Puppies (page 81).*

YIELD · 4 SERVINGS

FRIED PERCH

2 *fresh perch*

1–2 *cups vegetable oil*

2–4 *tablespoons butter*

1/2 *cup fine, white cornmeal*

1/2 *teaspoon salt*

1/4 *teaspoon pepper*

Each lake spread out over the Houghton Ranch is a beautiful oasis in itself. Set on the open range, they water stock, store water for irrigation of the Ranch gardens and orchards, and of course, exist as natural magnets for the plentiful wildlife of the High Plains. The fishing is excellent; the lakes are full of perch, bass, and catfish. During the summer, hardly a day goes by that someone doesn't fill his creel at one "hole" or another.

One visitor was Joe Scott of Dalhart, a close family friend and one of Ted Houghton's fishing buddies. Every so often he'd arrive early in the morning, and by 11:00 A.M. he'd be down at the creek by the Headquarters cleaning a bunch of perch for Nanny's lunchtime fish fry.

Fried crisp and crunchy with fine, white cornmeal, the perch were served with hush puppies, hot buttered corn on the cob, and a large platter of thick-sliced beefsteak tomatoes and sweet Ranch-raised Bermuda onions. A hot cobbler served with rich, lumpy cream would top off this happy meal.

It's so easy to recall Nanny's satisfaction with this particular meal, for she never failed to say how much she liked fish fresh from the lake. I think her pleasure hovered between appreciation for fresh fish and the idea that something so good came from her own "backyard" —even if the lake in her own "backyard" was on the Ranch 2 miles away!

METHOD

Clean the perch, removing the scales, heads, and entrails. Rinse and pat dry. Put enough oil in a frying pan to come halfway up the fish when both are in the pan. The fish should not touch each other. Add the butter and heat the oil-butter mixture over moderately high heat until a cube of bread will fry immediately (350°F).

Dredge the perch in the cornmeal seasoned with salt and pepper.

Measure the thickness of the perch at the thickest part and cook the fish for a total time of about 5 minutes per ½"; in other words, 2½ minutes per side if ½" thick. Fry the fish in the hot oil until crisp and brown, turning once, and turning heat down to moderate. Drain on paper towels and serve immediately.

YIELD · 2 SERVINGS

PAN-FRIED TROUT

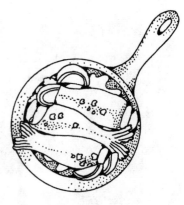

A day's drive from the Ranch, the mountain streams of Colorado teem with rainbow, cutthroat, and Dolly Vorden trout. Ted Houghton and his many friends often took off to "Eagle's Nest," where they had cabins and lots of good times and, as family snapshots of those outings show, caught a lot of fish. The recipe below for fried trout is classic. To enjoy trout at its best, though, the bones should be removed according to the instructions given below.

METHOD

Gut the trout and rinse well. Gently pat dry.

Put enough oil in a frying pan to come halfway up the fish when both are in the pan. The fish should not touch each other. Heat the oil over moderately high heat until a cube of bread will fry immediately (350°F).

Roll the trout in the flour seasoned with salt and pepper and gently pat the flour on.

INGREDIENTS

2 trout

1–2 cups vegetable oil

1 cup all-purpose flour

1 teaspoon salt

½ teaspoon pepper

2 tablespoons butter

2 tablespoons minced fresh parsley

½ lemon, unsliced

½ lemon, sliced

Measure the thickness of the trout at the thickest part and cook the fish about 10 minutes per measured inch, or 5 minutes per side if 1″ thick, 7½ minutes per side if 1½″ thick. Fry in the hot oil, turning once. If the trout is thicker than 1 inch, cook on its back for a minute or two, holding it with a pair of tongs.

To bone the cooked fish, put it on its side with the head facing to your left. Stick the point of a sharp knife in the trout's flesh just to the left of its tail and gently move the blade over its backbone to the left toward the fish's head. When your knife reaches the open rib cage, gently push the fish onto its back with a fork, then steady it with the knife. Now, place the fork inside the trout's rib cage and begin to "comb" the flesh on the far side of the fish away from the bones and onto the plate. When all the flesh is combed off the bones and has fallen to the plate, pick up the fish's head, tug gently to the right, and the entire rib cage will come right off. Check for any remaining bones and pour on your pan sauce of melted butter, chopped parsley, and a little lemon. As Alva T. said about Chile Con Queso, "Once you get the hang of it, it'll be just like comin' home to dinner."

To make the pan sauce, pour off all the oil from the pan. Over low heat, add the butter and chopped parsley. Gently scrape the pan with a wooden spoon to loosen fried particles. Stir constantly until the butter is melted. Squeeze the lemon once or twice over the mixture and stir. Pour sauce over boned fish that have been arranged on warm dinner plates. Garnish with the lemon slices. Serve immediately.

YIELD · 2 SERVINGS

POACHED TROUT

 If you have fresh trout but can't eat them right away, this recipe makes a cool, tasty lunch that can be enjoyed a day or two later.

M E T H O D

Gut the trout and rinse well.

In a pan large enough to hold the trout side by side, bring to a boil enough water to just cover trout, adding the onion, salt, and pepper. Lay the trout in the pan, lay a sheet of foil over, and gently simmer the trout, turning once halfway through cooking. Cook the fish for a total of about 10 minutes per measured inch at its thickest part, 5 minutes per side if 1″ thick, 7½ minutes per side if 1½″ thick. Remove from the water when done, chill, bone (see Pan-Fried Trout, page 99), and serve cold with mayonnaise.

NOTE: *Cold poached trout also makes an unusual hors d'oeuvre or first course. First, debone the poached trout as described in the recipe for Pan-Fried Trout (page 99). Then, place 2 or 3 tablespoons mayonnaise where the fish's head was and arrange toast points and lemon around the perimeter of the planked trout. Pieces of the fish, placed on the toast points and seasoned with a bit of mayonnaise and a few drops of lemon juice, are especially pleasing if the trout has been just poached and barely cooled to room temperature. For appetizer servings, one-half fish is sufficient.*

YIELD · 2 SERVINGS

INGREDIENTS

2 trout

1 medium onion, sliced

1 tablespoon salt

½ tablespoon peppercorns

2 tablespoons mayonnaise

FOURTH OF JULY BARBECUE, ABOUT 1934

BARBECUE

Three years into their venture, the Ranch was so successful that Lee decided he wanted to buy Reynolds out. Lee wired his partner, who had returned to Denver, to come down to the Ranch right away. On arrival, Lee informed Reynolds of an imminent takeover. But Reynolds surprised Lee and said he'd do the buying. Well, Lee gave him ten days to put up the money, assuming it was impossible. And that's when the excitement began.

Reynolds galloped off to the nearest railroad in Trinidad, Colorado, where he caught a train east. In New York, he found a backer and returned, much to Lee's astonishment, just in time to buy the Ranch. The two never exchanged a kind word again.

Reynolds was joined by his brother, and they ran this "outfit" for twenty years. Then, in 1902, they sold out to a Scottish-English syndicate called the "Prairie Land and Cattle Company."

Nowadays, you can get to the Ranch from New York in "just" ten hours; a trip I happily make whenever I can. One of the things I look forward to when I get there is barbecue. Brisket or ribs slow-baked over mesquite served with Nanny's sweet, tangy sauce are my favorites. For variety, however, I've included recipes for chicken and shrimp as well.

Of course, if you want to get a firsthand sample of real Panhandle barbecue, there's always the XIT Rodeo & Reunion's "free feed" barbecue. Every year, on the first Saturday in August, the great folks of Dalhart serve their barbecue free to twenty thousand fans and competitors who come to their town for the world's largest amateur rodeo. It takes 12,000 pounds of barbecued beef, 800 pounds of pinto beans, 600 pounds of onions, 250 loaves of bread, 40 gallons of pickles, and 48 gallons of applesauce. So, for the price of dinner for two at New York's ultra-haute Lutèce, you can get an advance-purchase, discounted round-trip air ticket to Amarillo, rent a car, and drive out to Dalhart to enjoy some free barbecue with a lot of folks who will be glad to see you!

Barbecued Beef

Salt and pepper

3 *pounds lean brisket*

1½ *cups Nanny's "J.J." Barbecue Marinade (page 183)*

1⅓ *cups Nanny's "J.J." Barbecue Sauce (page 177)*

You can't have a ranch without a barbecue. The Houghton Ranch has its big one on the Fourth of July when family and friends come out to the Headquarters in droves to feast on barbecued brisket and Nanny's special sauce. Fortunately, though, this version is easy to make, so it's enjoyed far more often than just once a year. Traditionally, brisket is wrapped in moistened burlap, buried in a pit full of coals, and baked for 24 hours. In the version here, well-marinated beef is seared on a covered grill, sealed in foil, and then slow-baked until it's tender enough to eat with a fork. The result is incredibly close to real pit barbecue and a lot easier to make.

Before serving, the brisket should be sliced thin across the grain and reheated with Barbecue Sauce. At the Ranch, Lillie places the slices in a baking dish and generously covers them with sauce before warming. I prefer to put just a dollop or two of sauce on each slice, and then stack them neatly in foil packages wrapped tightly for reheating. This keeps the meat juicy but does not obscure the smoky, crispy edges of the seared meat.

METHOD

Salt and pepper the brisket generously—there should be twice as much pepper on the meat as salt. Marinate the brisket in the marinade for at least 2 hours at room temperature. (If the weather is very hot, refrigerate and marinate for 4 hours. Return to room temperature before cooking.)

Remove the brisket from the marinade.

Broil over white-hot mesquite coals, covered, until crisp and seared on both sides, 15 to 20 minutes per side. Remove, paint all sides with the barbecue sauce, and wrap in aluminum foil. Place in the oven set to the lowest temperature (200°F) and bake for at least 6 hours. *(cont.)*

Remove the meat and thinly slice. Place a dollop of barbecue sauce between each slice, wrap in foil again and warm before serving. Do not warm the slices more than 30–45 minutes. Overcooking will make the sauce too sweet.

YIELD · 6 SERVINGS

BARBECUED CHICKEN

If you like to include chicken in your barbecue, try Martha Houghton's Barbecue Marinade and her Barbecue Sauce. It works wonders under the broiler or on the grill.

INGREDIENTS

2   1½-pound broilers, quartered
    Salt and pepper

2   cups Nanny's "J.J." Barbecue Marinade (page 183)

2   cups Nanny's "J.J." Barbecue Sauce (page 177)

METHOD

Place the chicken pieces in a noncorrodible container and pour the marinade over. Sprinkle with a little salt and generously with pepper. Marinate, covered, for 2 to 3 hours at room temperature. If the weather is hot or humid, double the marinating time in the refrigerator. Drain the chicken well before barbecuing.

To cook indoors, place the chicken about 5 inches under the broiler, skin side down. Broil for 10 minutes, turn, and baste with the marinade. Broil for 10 minutes more. Turn, paint with the barbecue sauce, broil for 5 minutes. Turn again, paint with more sauce, and broil for 5 minutes more, or until the juice of the chicken runs clear when the thigh is pierced with a fork.

To cook outdoors, prepare a charcoal fire. When the coals are ready, place the chicken on the grill, cavity side down, for 10 minutes. Turn and cook, skin side down, for 5 minutes. Paint the cavity with the barbecue sauce. Turn again and cook for 5 minutes. Paint skin side with the sauce, turn, and cook, skin side down, 5 minutes more, or until the juice from the thigh runs clear when pierced with a fork.

NOTE: *Placing the chicken closer to the broiler before adding the barbecue sauce will reduce the amount of cooking time approximately 5 minutes per side. However, after painting the chicken pieces with the sauce, you should lower the rack because the sauce scorches very quickly.*

YIELD · 4 SERVINGS

BARBECUED SHRIMP

Martha Houghton never served barbecued shrimp. However, I'm willing to bet that if she tried them with her own Barbecue Marinade and Sauce, she'd have called Galveston often to have shrimp sent up to the Ranch via air express.

INGREDIENTS

2 *pounds large or jumbo "green" shrimp, peeled and deveined*

1½ *cups Nanny's "J.J." Barbecue Marinade (page 183)*

1 *cup Nanny's "J.J." Barbecue Sauce (page 177)*

METHOD

Place the shrimp in a noncorrodible container, cover with the marinade, and allow to sit, covered, at room temperature for 1 hour. In hot or humid weather, refrigerate for 2 hours.

Place the shrimp on a wire rack in a broiler pan. Paint the shrimp with barbecue sauce, sparingly. Place under the hot broiler for 3 to 5 minutes, depending on the size of the shrimp. Turn and paint again sparingly. Broil for another 3 to 5 minutes, or until the shrimp's flesh turns "white" all the way through. Do not overcook; the shrimp cooks very fast. If broiled too long, they will become dry and tough.

YIELD · 6 SERVINGS

BARBECUED SPARE RIBS

3–4 *pounds pork ribs,*
depending on
amount of meat
on bones

Salt and pepper
to taste

2 *cups Nanny's*
"J.J." Barbecue
Marinade (page
183)

1 *cup Nanny's*
"J.J." Barbecue
Sauce
(page 177)

The secret to these ribs is the marinade. The brown sugar and Worcestershire glaze the ribs dark and crisp. Grilling them over mesquite adds a sharp, woodsy flavor, but if you want sweeter ribs, just bake them in the oven. Either way, they're quite pleasing.

M E T H O D

Rinse and pat the ribs dry. Salt and pepper them generously. Paint the ribs with the marinade, cover and set aside for 2 hours at room temperature. If the weather is too hot, marinate in the refrigerator for 4 hours and then allow the ribs to return to room temperature briefly before cooking.

Preheat the oven to 500°F. Place the ribs on a rack in a roasting pan, place in the oven, and turn the oven down at once to 325°. Bake for 45 minutes, basting with the marinade every 10 to 15 minutes. Paint the ribs with barbecue sauce, and bake for another 15 minutes; paint again, and bake for 15 minutes more. The total cooking time is 1¼ hours.

If desired, after 45 minutes in the oven, you may finish the ribs over a barbecue grill. The hot coals should be covered with white ash and the ribs should be set at least 2 inches above them. For a smokier taste, grill the ribs covered. Paint the ribs every 15 minutes. Depending on the heat from your coals, the additional cooking time should take 30 to 45 minutes, for a total time of 1¼ to 1½ hours. For meatier ribs (the thick end of the rack usually has a flap, making the meat an inch or more thick), add 20 to 30 minutes cooking time. The ribs should develop a nice crust, and the juice should run clear when pricked with a fork.

YIELD · 4 SERVINGS

MESQUITE STEAKS

Up until recently, the idea that this low-growing shrub was good for anything would, at best, produce a hoot and a holler. Cowboys have cut it down, pulled it up, burned it, sprayed it, and cursed it as long as men and cattle have competed with it for water and land in the Lone Star State. Its thorny presence makes roping and herding next to impossible; its need for water is greater than several head of cattle. Indeed, mesquite is a thirsty shrub known to soak in up to 40 gallons of water per day. Where mesquite has been removed along riverbanks and breaks, the surrounding terrain has actually become greener and the water level higher.

On the treeless plains, however, mesquite provided wood for chuck-wagon fires that burned hotter and smelled better than buffalo chips. Later its intense heat and flavor made it the favorite fuel for barbecues. As for heat, mesquite burns so hot, people swear it will melt a frying pan. So, needless to say, it's great for searing meat. As for flavor, its woodsy aroma has captured the imagination of some of America's most innovative chefs, and now fetches prices in New York and Chicago that are equally heady. The flavor of mesquite, however, varies by species of which there are believed to be about thirty. Only two, "velvet" and "honey," are considered appropriate for cooking. The mesquite on the Houghton Ranch is of the honey variety and imparts a wonderful buttery, cedarlike aroma to foods grilled or smoked over it.

For mesquite, the "stands" or groves at the Ranch are relatively young, less than 100 years old and 3 to 5 feet high. In fact, most of the mesquite in the Panhandle is about this age, and is believed to have gained a foothold on the High Plains during the great cattle drives of the last century. Cattle driven from the southern part of

INGREDIENTS

4 *shell or loin steaks (or 2–3 pounds any good cut of steak, such as sirloin, London broil, or round)*

2 *cloves garlic, halved*

4–5 *mesquite chunks*

Kosher salt

Freshly ground pepper

Texas (where mesquite grows 2 stories high) ate the seeds of this shrub along their long, long trek north to Kansas. The seeds were replanted through cattle droppings, and over many years the mesquite slowly made its way north to the top of the Panhandle and beyond as new herds of cattle grazed on new stands of mesquite and then moved on.

At the Ranch, a charcoal fire is built in a barbecue pit and then wet pieces of mesquite are thrown on the fire to create aromatic smoke. A hood is lowered over the grill and heavily peppered meat is smoked as it is grilled. The result is steak that bites back.

Smoking and peppering should be done to taste. Smoking can be controlled by the amount of time the steak is allowed to cook covered.

METHOD

Soak four or five 2″ mesquite chunks in water for 1 hour.

Rub each steak with a garlic half. Sprinkle salt on the fatty edges and bone (if any). Generously pepper the meaty surfaces. Place the mesquite chunks on hot coals. Put the steaks on the grill. Turn once. See Note below for cooking times. Cover the grill briefly for more pronounced mesquite flavor. For gas grills, put the chunks in an aluminum pan before placing directly on lava rocks.

NOTE: *As a rule of thumb for steaks 1″ thick: for rare steaks, cook for a total of 6 minutes or until, when the steaks are pierced, the tines of a fork emerge barely warm. For medium-cooked steaks, grill for 7 to 8 minutes. When the steaks are pierced, the tines of a fork should be warm and the juice pink. For well-done steaks, grill for 10 minutes or more, or until, when the steaks are pierced, the tines of the fork emerge hot and the juice runs clear. This assumes steaks are placed 3″ to 4″ over coals.*

For parties, Nanny used this recipe to cook whole tenderloins, which were then sliced thin and served with hot biscuits, barbecue sauce, and thin-sliced Bermuda onions.

YIELD · 4 SERVINGS

WILD GAME

In 1915, Martha Houghton's father John M. Shelton acquired the Old "LE" from the Prairie Land and Cattle Company, a Scottish-English syndicate that had renamed the Ranch the "J.J." He paid them $3.50 an acre for 221,000 acres and obtained another 111,000 from the famed XIT Ranch by purchasing its "Bravo" Division, locally known as the "Best of the Best."

The Ranch was John Shelton's million-dollar reward at the end of a long, hard trail. Born poor in Kentucky, he built a fortune out of nothing but hard work. In Fort Worth, at age twelve, John made his first money by riding out onto the frozen range and skinning hides from cattle that had died in a

great blizzard. Before long, young Shelton had raised enough money to buy a small herd of his own and establish his brand, a letter *J* on its side—the Lazy J."

Shelton's father, however, had other plans for his son and apprenticed him to a druggist. Reluctantly, the boy left the wide-open spaces for the confines of a store. Two years later, though, Shelton managed to return to the range and acquired a new herd of cattle. Buying, selling, and trading cattle and land, he found his way to Amarillo and the Ranch.

Shelton's last range turned out to be as good for game as it is for cattle. With the exception of the buffalo, every animal and bird known to inhabit the High Plains thrived there, as they still do. Today, good forage and cover continue to draw far more than just deer or antelope to this well-watered range. Just one source, a big spring hidden in a draw at the rim of the broad and shallow Romero Canyon, attracts and supports all kinds of flora and fauna. First, it bubbles up cool and clear under the shade of cottonwoods, which are surrounded by a thicket of hackberry trees, ash, scrub oak, and Russian olive. Then, the spring is channeled into three lakes that are stepped into the side of the canyon. At the lowest lake, the water drains into a creek that moves down a gentle slope to irrigate the oasis and meander past the Headquarters. Finally, the creek winds its way into a lush pasture called "Million Dollar" where it empties into a lake before returning to the ground. In all, the Romero Creek flows for eight miles, and some incredible scenes in nature take place along the way.

The water in the spring is so cold, the perch that swim up from the first lake to nest and feed among the watercress come up just so far, and then suddenly dart and turn back. In the warmer lake water, huge bass lurk among the algae and rushes that grow along its western edges. Tufted kingfishers perched in willows wait ready to plunge for fish, their uneven wingbeats sounding like changing gears.

The lower lake is the largest and offers the best fishing. Large catfish slumber in the dark waters near the rushes as perch and blue gill sun themselves in the shallows near the western bank. Turtles float here and there or bask on stumps or limbs from trees that have fallen at the edges of the lake from exposure to decades of storms and strong winds.

The view from the western bank is spectacular. The long view of the Romero Canyon stretches for miles until the red earth and muted greens and tans of the range grass dissolve into the gray-blue horizon. In December, the sunsets take on a fiery hue. Then, at late dusk, it is not uncommon to see great flying wedges of Canada geese, ghostly silhouettes honking across the sky as they move in resolution to the east and literally into the edge of night.

The creek pushes its way down a gentle slope, and before long reaches the cow pens and the edge of the oasis where less wary wildlife make their home—doves, cottontails, skunk. Past the cow pens, white-tailed deer may be browsing in the apple orchards. In winter, at dusk, they wend their way across the creek, leap the barbed-wire fence in the "trap," or horse pasture, and leap out again to amble on in their stately, shy fashion to bed down in a fallow melon patch warmed by the low winter sun. Throughout the year, the orchards and gardens are their favorite haunts. In spring and summer, the deer play mild havoc with the corn and lettuce. In the fall, they enjoy a fine diet of all kinds of apples and pears. The deer are far from alone; raccoon, cottontails, and flocks of blackbirds just as often raid the gardens for midnight snacks.

The creek finally passes through one more thicket and flows out from the southern edge of the oasis. Here, the red-faced Mexican eagle is sometimes seen perched on the branch of an ash tree or the top of a post as it surveys the surrounding prairie. As it leaves the thicket, the creek enters the Million Dollar pasture thick with grasses and wild sunflowers. The grass and wildflowers are so profuse, it makes one wonder if this sight could have inspired Coronado's famous description of the Plains as a "sea of grasses."

Finally, in the middle of Million Dollar, the Romero Creek empties into a miragelike lake that's so close to the level bottom of the canyon that it sometimes seems to disappear from sight. In spite of its stark openness, the wildlife are at ease. Coyote, those nocturnal prowler-howlers, trot down the cow paths, prairie chickens pick among the "sea of grasses," and mule deer browse the wild sage. For some reason, pin-tailed ducks, as well as a few mergansers, seem to prefer the open water of Million Dollar lake.

It is little wonder that with wildlife and country like this, Ted Houghton was a conservationist as well as a

WHITE-TAILED DEER ON THE ROMERO CREEK,
JUNE 1931

TED HOUGHTON WITH HIS GRANDSON
WALTY CALDWELL, OCTOBER 1953

hunter and fisherman. There are those who recall that he was not an avid hunter. However, if he didn't shoot much, he didn't miss much, either—as a result, when Nanny and Unc inherited the J.J. Division of the Ranch in 1923, they became as committed to maintaining the wildlife on their spread as they were to maintaining the "Lazy J" brand.

The recipes presented here are really an interpretation of how Martha Houghton cooked what was bagged at the Ranch or on fishing and hunting trips. There weren't many recipes for game in her collections—probably because, to her, preparing game was second nature. Basically, most recipes focus on the flavors Nanny considered appropriate for game such as apple and sage. These recipes also reflect her love of black pepper and onion as well as cooking game by frying, broiling, and smothering.

VENISON

ANTELOPE OR VENISON STEAKS

Come October, neighbors and friends gather at the Headquarters for the yearly antelope hunt. It's the high point of the shooting season and the chance to bag what it takes to make these peppery steaks with their rich, creamy sauce. If you can't get antelope, venison will easily do. In fact, having tried this recipe on venison, I'd have to say it's a great way to prepare a cut that is frequently tough and gamy.

METHOD

Place the steaks in a pan and pour the marinade over. Marinate for 2 to 3 hours at room temperature, or 4 to 6 hours in the refrigerator.

Remove the steaks from the marinade and pat dry. Reserve the marinade. Rub the steaks with the garlic halves and sprinkle the steaks heavily on both sides with the pepper. Pound the pepper into the surfaces with the flat side of a meat cleaver or heavy knife.

Melt the lard or bacon drippings in a heavy skillet over high heat. Place the steaks in the pan, turn heat down to medium-high, and cook for 2 to 3 minutes on each side, depending on the thickness, turning just once, for rare to medium rare. Remove the steaks from the pan and keep warm.

Pour off all but 1 tablespoon of fat from the pan. Add the onion and fry until lightly browned. Pour in 1 cup of the

INGREDIENTS

2–3 pounds antelope or venison steaks or chops, sliced 3/4"–1" thick

2 cups Red Game Marinade (page 184)

2 cloves garlic, halved

Freshly coarse-ground black pepper

4–5 tablespoons lard or bacon drippings

1/2 cup chopped onions

1 tablespoon butter

2 tablespoons flour

1 cup beef broth

2 tablespoons heavy cream

Salt

reserved marinade, stir to deglaze the pan, and boil until reduced by half.

Meanwhile, in a saucepan, melt the butter and stir in the flour until smooth. Add the reduced marinade, stirring, and stir in the beef broth until smooth. Bring to a boil, simmer for 5 minutes, add the cream and simmer a minute longer. Correct seasoning and serve hot.

YIELD · 4–6 SERVINGS

VENISON BURGERS
Also good for pork or red game

 Ground venison is a precious ingredient when it comes to chili. In fact, some "chiliheads" jealously hoard their supply and swear it's downright "catalytic." However, if you're open to trying your own ground venison in anything else, these burgers are well worth the risk.

Here, Nanny cleverly modified a beef recipe, clipped from Lord knows where, and as usual, the result is simple and elegant. The combination of marjoram and onion mingles with the venison well and the bay leaf adds an aromatic, luxurious touch. These burgers also keep lean meat reasonably moist, and are equally good for lean game such as antelope or elk. You can even make them with pork; just take care to cook the patties completely.

INGREDIENTS

1 1/2 pounds ground venison or coarsely ground pork

1/2 teaspoon salt

1/2 teaspoon pepper

1/4 teaspoon onion powder

3/4 teaspoon dried marjoram

1 egg, beaten

1 1/2 teaspoons vegetable oil

1 1/2 teaspoons butter or bacon drippings

6 bay leaves

METHOD

In a bowl, mix the meat, seasonings, and egg well, using your hands, and shape into 6 patties.

Grease a frying pan with the vegetable oil, and brown the patties over high heat, for 2 minutes on each side. While the second side is browning, place a bay leaf on each patty. Then turn heat down to low, turn the patties, add butter or bacon drippings, and cook slowly for 3 minutes more on the bay leaf side for the venison, 7 to 8 minutes for the pork; turn once more and cook for another 3 minutes on the other side for medium-rare venison and 7 to 8 minutes for the pork, or until the juices run clear. Bacon drippings are recommended for pork because butter cooked this long may burn or discolor and smoke. Serve immediately with the bay leaves on top, but discard them before eating.

YIELD · 6 SERVINGS

VENISON ROAST

Made the following way, venison becomes surprisingly tender and mild. Some might even say it tastes like a four-legged creature that's never mentioned at the Ranch, let alone served. Indeed, lamb hasn't been eaten here since the Spanish sheepherders who grazed their sheep on the High Plains returned to Santa Fe in the late 1870s.

METHOD

Place the roast in a pan and pour the marinade over. Marinate for 4 to 6 hours in the refrigerator.

Preheat the oven to 375°F.

Remove the venison from the marinade and pat dry. Reserve 2 cups of the marinade. Scrape any visible fat from the venison. Rub the meat all over with the garlic clove, then cut the clove in small slivers. Pierce the meat all over with a meat fork or sharp paring knife and insert the garlic slivers at random into the holes. Sprinkle the rosemary and pepper over the roast and rub into the surface of the meat.

INGREDIENTS

3–4 pounds venison roast

4 cups Red Game Marinade (page 184)

1 clove garlic, halved

1/2 tablespoon dried rosemary, crushed

Pepper

1/4 pound pork fatback

2 tablespoons butter

2 tablespoons flour

1 cup beef broth

Place the roast on a rack in a roasting pan. Cut the fatback into thin sheets and lay over the roast. Pour the reserved marinade into the pan. Place in the oven and roast for 20 to 25 minutes per pound for medium rare, or to 130° to 135° degrees on a meat thermometer. Baste with the pan juices every 15 minutes. Remove the fatback about 20 minutes before the roast is done to let the meat brown. Remove the roast from the pan and let sit. Remove and save all the liquid from the pan.

In a saucepan melt the butter. Stir in the flour until smooth, then add 1 cup of the pan juices and the broth, stirring to loosen the pan glaze. Simmer for 5 minutes, until smooth and thickened.

YIELD · 6—8 SERVINGS

DUCK

FRIED MALLARD BREASTS

For years, Martha and Ted Houghton traveled south in the winter to shoot duck on the Texas gulf. "They were so plentiful," Nanny often recalled, "we just ate the breasts fried in bacon."

Frying these breasts make them a little moister than broiling. The best part about this recipe, though, is the sauce. Rich and smoky with bacon and apples, it's a terrific foil for gamy, wild duck. You'll need 2 days, though, to allow the duck to marinate.

M E T H O D

Place the duck breasts in a pan and pour the marinade over; let marinate in the refrigerator for 2 days. Remove the breasts from the marinade and pat dry.

Fry the bacon until crisp in a large heavy skillet and drain on paper towels. Drain off all but 2 tablespoons of the fat. Reserve the drained fat. Sauté the onion over low heat until translucent. Remove with a slotted spoon and set aside. Sauté the duck breasts over medium heat, skin side down, for 4 to 5 minutes, turn over, and sauté for another 4 to 5 minutes, or until the juices are rosy-pink. Remove the duck and keep warm.

Add 1 tablespoon of the reserved fat to the skillet. Stir the flour into the fat in the skillet until smooth. Add the cider and water, stirring, and cook until thickened and smooth. Crumble the bacon and add, along with the onion, to the sauce. Season with salt and pepper to taste, simmer for 5 minutes, and serve at once with the duck.

INGREDIENTS

2 *mallard duck breasts, boned but not skinned*

1½ *cups Marinade for Waterfowl (page 184)*

4 *strips bacon*

¾ *cup chopped onion*

1 *tablespoon flour*

½ *cup apple cider*

½ *cup water*

Salt and pepper

YIELD · 2–3 SERVINGS

GRILLED MALLARD

This recipe takes some advance preparation—2 days—but it's worth the extra effort. The marinated mallard breasts broil quickly and contrast quite well with the easily made sauce that smacks of wild plums and sage.

INGREDIENTS

2 *mallard duck breasts, boned but not skinned*

1½ *cups Marinade for Waterfowl (page 184)*

1 *tablespoon butter*

1 *small clove garlic, minced*

1½ *tablespoons flour*

½ *teaspoon ground sage*

1 *cup game or chicken stock*

1 *tablespoon plum or currant jelly*

½ *tablespoon red wine vinegar*

Salt and pepper

METHOD

Place the duck breasts in a pan and pour the marinade over; let marinate for 2 days in the refrigerator.

Preheat a grill, using mesquite chips per directions.

Remove the breasts from the marinade and pat dry; reserve ¼ cup of the marinade. Grill the duck over the mesquite, skin side down first, 4 to 5 minutes per side for medium rare, or grill under an indoor broiler, skin side up first, 4 to 5 minutes per side.

Meantime, melt the butter in a small saucepan. Sauté the garlic gently for a minute or two, then stir in the flour until smooth. Stir in the sage, then the reserved marinade and stock, and cook until smooth and thickened. Stir in the jelly and vinegar, and salt and pepper to taste. Simmer for 5 minutes, correct the seasoning, and serve at once with the duck breasts.

YIELD · 2–3 SERVINGS

ROAST MALLARD

Stuffing the duck with apple, onion, and a bay leaf can draw off some of its gaminess and also add a wonderful aroma. The stuffing can also retard the internal temperature of the bird so that the skin and bacon can cook long enough to achieve some crispness without drying out the duck. As for the sauce, the cider and jelly add a faintly sweet and tart edge to the pan gravy. For an interesting touch, add a few bits of diced apple from the roasted ducks.

M E T H O D

Preheat the oven to 450°F.

Rinse the ducks, inside and out; shake the water out of the cavity and pat the outside dry. Rub the inside of the cavity with salt and pepper. Place 2 wedges of apple, 1 bay leaf and 1 tablespoon onion inside each cavity. Sprinkle pepper over the outsides, and drape each duck with 2 bacon strips.

Pour the marinade into a roasting pan just large enough to hold the ducks. Place a rack in the pan and the ducks on the rack. Roast the ducks for 15 minutes. Turn the oven down to 325° and roast for 25 to 30 minutes for rare, 35 to 40 minutes for medium rare, or until the juices run rosy-pink when pricked with a meat fork. If the bacon cooks before the duck, remove it to some paper towels to drain, and serve later. After the bacon is removed, baste every 15 minutes until the duck is done.

When the ducks are done, set them aside and keep warm. Deglaze the roasting pan with the cider and set aside. Melt the butter in a saucepan, and stir in the flour. When smooth, pour in the cider mixture and stir until smooth. Add the jelly and chicken broth and bring to a boil. Simmer for 5 minutes, stir in the cream, and simmer a minute longer. Correct the seasoning and serve with the ducks.

YIELD · 4 SERVINGS

INGREDIENTS

2–3 mallard ducks, plucked and dressed

Salt and pepper

1 apple, cored and cut into 6 wedges

2–3 bay leaves

2–3 tablespoons chopped onion

4–6 strips bacon

1 cup Marinade for Waterfowl (page 184)

½ cup apple cider

2 tablespoons butter

2 tablespoons flour

1 tablespoon plum, apple, or currant jelly

1 cup chicken broth

2 tablespoons heavy cream

GAME BIRDS

PRAIRIE CHICKEN

If you can't bag a prairie chicken, a pheasant will do jut fine. The bacon used to "bard" or keep the game bird moist makes a terrific foil for this dish, so set the bacon aside as soon it's crisp and baste the bird with drippings until it's done. And oh, yes, be sure to save the frame for Sagebrush Soup!

INGREDIENTS

- *1 prairie chicken or pheasant, plucked and dressed*
- *1 quart milk*
- *¼ teaspoon salt*
- *1 bay leaf*
- *1 lemon wedge*
- *1 clove garlic, halved*
- *1 tablespoon poultry seasoning*
- *Pepper*
- *4 strips bacon*

METHOD

Soak the prairie chicken in the milk for 3 to 6 hours to tenderize. Remove from the milk, drain, and pat dry.

Preheat the oven to 400°F.

Sprinkle the salt in the cavity of the prairie chicken and rub in well. Place the bay leaf, lemon wedge, and garlic in the cavity. Rub the poultry seasoning into the skin and sprinkle with pepper to taste.

Place the prairie chicken on a rack in a roasting pan and drape the bacon over the bird. Roast for 15 minutes, then reduce heat to 350° and continue roasting. When the bacon is done, remove the strips and baste the bird every 10 to 15 minutes, until the juices run clear from a thigh, 50 to 60 minutes, depending on the size of the bird.

NOTE: *This recipe is suitable for other game birds such as chukar partridge or grouse. Cooking time should be approximately 18 to 20 minutes per pound.*

VARIATION: *Try the Game Sauce for Prairie Chicken (page 180) as an accompaniment to this dish.*

YIELD · 2–3 SERVINGS

FRIED DOVE OR QUAIL

Sometimes, the simplest way is the best way. In this part of the country, most people fry their dove. They fry a little bacon and onion, set the cooked bits aside, and fry their dove like chicken. Then, they serve them up with bacon and onion-flavored cream gravy. They're so good, folks in the Panhandle look forward to dove season all year long.

METHOD

Split the doves in half and soak in buttermilk for 2 hours at room temperature.

Heat a skillet and fry the bacon and onion until browned and crisp. Remove the pieces with a slotted spoon and reserve. Add enough vegetable oil to the grease in the pan to come halfway up the sides of the doves. Heat the oil to 375°F.

Remove the dove halves from the buttermilk and drain briefly on paper towels. Mix the 1 cup flour with 1 teaspoon each salt and pepper. Dredge the doves in the flour mixture and shake off any excess. Fry the doves in the hot oil, a few at a time, 2 to 3 minutes per side, until butterscotch brown and the juices run clear when the thigh is pricked with a skewer. Remove and drain on paper towels. Keep warm.

When all the doves are fried, drain off all but 1 tablespoon of the oil. Add the 2 tablespoons flour and stir until smooth. Add the cream, milk, and chicken broth and stir until smooth. Bring to a boil, stirring and scraping bits from the pan bottom, and simmer for 5 minutes, until thickened and smooth. Season to taste with salt and pepper.

Place the doves on a platter, sprinkle with the reserved bacon and onion bits, and serve the cream gravy separately.

INGREDIENTS

8 doves, or small quail, under 4 ounces each, cleaned and dressed

1 quart buttermilk

1/4 pound bacon, cut into 1/2" pieces

1 onion, cut into 1/2" pieces

Vegetable oil

1 cup all-purpose flour, plus 2 tablespoons

Salt and pepper

2/3 cup heavy cream

2/3 cup milk

1/2 cup chicken broth

YIELD · 4 SERVINGS

BROILED QUAIL

Mostly, quail are fried or sautéed. However, if the birds are large enough to offer as a modest single serving, they can also be broiled. Broiling, in this simple recipe, produces crispy skin and juicy meat. The lemon and rosemary impart a delicate flavor that make quail cooked this way light and elegant.

INGREDIENTS

8 quails, about 4 to 5 ounces each, cleaned and dressed

3 cloves garlic, minced

4 tablespoons olive oil

3 tablespoons lemon juice

2 teaspoons salt

1/2 teaspoon pepper

1 tablespoon dried crushed rosemary

1/4 pound butter, softened

1/2 cup game stock or chicken broth

1 tablespoon dry sherry

METHOD

Split the quails in half by cutting down the backbone. Remove or break the soft part of the breast bone, and flatten out spread-eagle fashion. Rinse and pat dry.

Mix the garlic, oil, lemon juice, salt, pepper, and rosemary in a glass or ceramic container just large enough to hold all the birds in one layer. Paint the birds on all sides with the mixture, cover the dish, and refrigerate overnight.

Preheat the broiler.

In a bowl whisk the butter, stock, and sherry together and paint the quail on all sides with the mixture. Place the quail on a rack in a broiling pan, skin side down, and broil for about 7 minutes. Turn the quail over, baste with the pan juices, and broil for about another 6 minutes, or until brown and the juices run clear when pierced with a meat fork. Small quail should take about 13 minutes in all, larger ones about 18 minutes.

NOTE: *This recipe can also accommodate 2- to 3-ounce doves quite nicely. However, they cook so fast, it is difficult to achieve crisp skin without drying them out. If you do try this recipe with doves, place them close to the broiler and cook them on each side for no more than 5 to 6 minutes per side. Turn your back on them at your own risk!*

YIELD · 8 SERVINGS

SMOTHERED QUAIL

If you like pheasant smitane or beef Strogan-off, you'll find this approach to quail quite pleasing. Quail are most often quick-fried, but for a more elegant meal, the birds are browned and then baked in their own pan gravy. Then, not too long before serving, sour cream is added to make the sauce rich and creamy.

METHOD

Preheat the oven to 350°F.

Split the quail down the backbone and spread flat, breaking or removing the breast bone with poultry shears or a sharp knife. Season the birds with the salt, pepper, and thyme. Dredge the quail in the 1 cup flour, patting the flour on heavily.

In a large frying pan, melt 4 tablespoons butter with the oil and sauté the birds over medium-high heat until light brown on both sides. Remove the birds from the pan. Discard the butter.

Melt the remaining butter in the frying pan and sauté the onion or shallots until lightly browned. Add the 2 table-spoons flour and stir until smooth. Add the stock and heat, stirring, until thick and smooth. Stir in the jelly until melted. Return the quail to the pan and cover with the sauce mixture. Cover and bake in the oven for 1 hour. Remove the cover, set the quail aside, and stir in the sour cream. Heat, stirring, until smooth and hot, but do not boil. Return the quail to the pan, baste with the sauce, and serve immediately.

YIELD · 8 SERVINGS

INGREDIENTS

- 8 quail, cleaned and dressed
- Salt and pepper to taste
- 1 teaspoon dried thyme
- 1 cup all-purpose flour, plus 2 tablespoons
- 6 tablespoons butter
- 2 tablespoons vegetable oil
- 1/3 cup finely chopped red onions or shallots
- 2 cups chicken or game stock
- 1 teaspoon Plum Jelly (page 62) or other tart jelly
- 1 cup sour cream, room temperature

TED HOUGHTON
(*3RD FROM LEFT*)
WHEN HE LED
GENERAL ''BLACK JACK''
PERSHING SOUTH
OF THE BORDER
AFTER PANCHO VILLA
IN 1916

TEX - MEX

In 1916, Ted Houghton led General "Black Jack" Pershing south of the Border into Old Mexico in search of Pancho Villa. Unc's father had ranches in Chihuahua, and so the story goes, he knew the territory like the back of his hand. Nevertheless, Unc was captured, but the bandit holding him prisoner had worked for his father as a vaquero. So, somehow, Unc talked the guard into letting him go.

If Unc hadn't come back, we might never have enjoyed his famous chili con queso or his classic "bowl of red." He loved Mexican food and didn't mind taking a turn or two in the kitchen to "get some up" for his friends.

However, chili is a controversial

subject in Texas and it seems as though everyone loves to get in the act. So there are four chili recipes to try— and to keep the peace, with beans or without; all venison; some venison or none; with tomatoes or without, and oh yes, even with bourbon.

The balance of the recipes in this chapter are not so controversial. They're reasonably simple versions of Tex-Mex classics such as enchiladas or guacamole, as much fun to make as they are to eat. The Chiles Rellenos and Sopaipillas are a bit more complicated, but they're worth the initial extra effort. Once you get to know them, these recipes are not at all intimidating.

ONE WAY OF
SETTLING
THE CHILI
CONTRO-
VERSY

Lastly, these recipes call for pure ground chile. However, they will turn out quite well even if only chili powder is available. Use pure ground chile if you can, though. Panhandle cooks use mild ground chile from New Mexico, and it does make a difference. If you must use commercial chili powder, do not add any salt until you taste what you've made. Also, corn flour (masa harina or masa repa) is an important ingredient used in Chili Gravy and Chiles Rellenos, added for flavor and texture. If you cannot get it, use more regular flour; you will need it to thicken the gravy.

CHILE CON QUESO

One of Uncle Ted's best-remembered party dishes, this recipe can easily be adjusted to serve one or many. As Alva T. describes its preparation, "Once you get the hang of it, it'll be just like comin' home to dinner!"

METHOD

Cut the tomatoes into ¼″ dice.

Melt the butter in a large heavy pot. Sauté the onion until translucent. Stir in the flour and cook, stirring, for 2 to 3 minutes. Stir in the tomatoes and chiles until blended. Add the cheese, and heat slowly, stirring, until the cheese is just melted and warm. Add the Worcestershire and Tabasco, and taste for seasoning. Serve warm with chips or crackers.

NOTE: *It is important to heat the cheese slowly; if it is heated too fast or too long, it will break down and separate.*

YIELD · 6—8 SERVINGS

INGREDIENTS

1 16-ounce can whole tomatoes, drained, halved and seeded

2 tablespoons butter

1 softball-size Spanish onion, chopped

1—2 tablespoons flour

4 4-ounce cans chopped green chiles, drained

2½ pounds extra-sharp Cheddar cheese (preferably white), shredded

½ teaspoon Worcestershire sauce

¼ teaspoon Tabasco sauce

Tortilla chips or saltines

CHILES RELLENOS

There's a special place on my palate and in my heart for these deep-fried chiles. At least once a week, we'd drive 40 miles to Dalhart for supper at Trinidad and Della's Mexican café. Lodged in a faded blue-and-white stucco drive-in, a flashing 7-UP sign and rows of Cadillacs and pickup trucks parked outside were the only outward signs of life. Inside, though, the atmosphere was festive, to say the least. Old Trinidad would be sitting near the door, chain smoking and greeting his guests with his big, wizened smile. His wife Della would be manning the kitchen, turning out some of the best Tex-Mex specialties I've had anywhere. Meanwhile, assorted members of their family cheerfully waited on a full house.

Neon signs for Coors Banquet Beer, velvet sombreros, and gaudy tapestries hung on dark blue walls. Yellow formica tables set with bright blue plastic glasses under fluorescent lights set the stage for Della's colorful food. Big groups like ours would put two or three tables together and settle in for a lot of beer and a lot of laughs. Young cowboys with their wives and babies, teen-agers on dates, older folk, town fathers, or lone truckers perched on stools at the counter, would wander in and out, all totally satisfied for $3 or $4 a head.

Sad to say, Trinidad and Della are now retired. However, these chile rellenos will give you an idea of what we enjoyed. Most versions call for a fluffy batter, but this one produces a thin, crunchy coating that tastes of toasted corn without interfering with the subtle flavors of sweet chiles and cheese.

Once you get the knack of frying pepper, you'll find these chiles easy to make and delicious when served with enchiladas or huevos rancheros. The method below calls for roasting the peppers until they blister.

However, the *Joy of Cooking*—one of Nanny's favorite kitchen tomes—suggests deep-frying at 375°F. for 30 seconds, which is faster. If you want to try this approach, the fat needed for frying the chiles rellenos should be adequate.

NOTE: Hope Farrell, who tested these recipes, made a wonderful discovery when she made these chiles rellenos. The batter looked just like the kind used for pancakes. She found that adding a teaspoon of baking powder to a cup of leftover batter just before cooking makes terrific cornmeal pancakes. To quote Hope, "They're quite nice." Great with Nanny's brandy sauce, these cornmeal cakes, made in miniature sizes, even have dessert potential with whipped cream and praline sauce. A cup of batter makes six 4" pancakes or twelve 2" pancakes.

METHOD

Roast the chiles on gas trivets or place on a rack and pan under a broiler and turn with tongs frequently until the skin is blistered. Place the chiles in a brown paper bag, close up and cool. Remove the chiles from the bag, remove the skins, but do not remove the stems. Make a small, vertical slit just below each stem and remove the seeds. Insert a strip of cheese into each chile.

Pour the oil 2" deep in a skillet and heat to 375°F.

In a bowl mix the masa, flour, cornmeal, baking powder, and salt well. Beat the eggs with the milk and stir into the dry ingredients, mixing well. If the mixture becomes too thick as it stands, add a little more milk—the consistency should be that of pancake batter. Coat the chiles with the batter and lower by the stems or with tongs into the hot oil. Deep-fry for 2½ to 3 minutes, or until golden brown. Remove with a slotted spoon and drain on paper towels. Serve immediately with a small bowl of Gar's Chili Salsa or green picante salsa at the table.

YIELD · 6 SERVINGS

INGREDIENTS

- 6 *mild green chiles (or Italian frying peppers) with stems*
- 6 *ounces Monterey Jack cheese, cut into 6 strips*
- *Vegetable oil for frying*
- ½ *cup masa harina or masa repa*
- ½ *cup granulated flour for gravies and coatings*
- 1 *cup yellow cornmeal*
- 1 *teaspoon baking powder*
- ¼ *teaspoon salt*
- 2 *eggs*
- 1½ *cups milk*
- *Gar's Chile Salsa (page 181) or green picante salsa (available commercially)*

CHILI GRAVY

*1 tablespoon lard or
 bacon drippings*

*1½ tablespoons masa
 harina or masa
 repa*

*1 tablespoon yellow
 cornmeal*

*1 clove garlic,
 crushed*

*⅛ teaspoon ground
 cumin*

*⅛ teaspoon dried
 oregano*

*2 tablespoons
 ground chiles or
 chili powder*

*2 cups beef broth
 Salt*

If French chefs have their basic brown sauce, Tex-Mex cooks have their chili gravy. It's the sauce that makes the difference on the Huevos Rancheros, Enchilada Stacks, or Enchiladas con Queso mentioned in this book.

Since the level of salt and spiciness may vary in the chili powder you use, it's best to leave out the salt initially and season to taste when the gravy is done. If you can get mild plain ground chile, so much the better. You'll avoid the possibility of saltiness and get a gravy that has a sharper, cleaner flavor.

METHOD

Heat the lard or drippings in a frying pan and slowly sauté the masa, cornmeal, garlic, cumin, and oregano until golden brown. Add the chili powder and then the broth, slowly, stirring until the mixture is smooth and bubbly. Simmer, uncovered, for 10 minutes, then cover and simmer for another 10 to 15 minutes. Add salt to taste, if desired.

YIELD · 1 ½ — 1 ¾ CUPS

MOM'S CHILI CON CARNE

My mother and Nanny swapped recipes for almost 40 years. At some point, they must have covered the controversial subject of chili because Mom's favorite recipe turned up in Nanny's extensive collection. I say "controversial" because the addition of beans to chili is hotly debated by Lone Star cooks committed to turning out the ultimate "bowl of red."

This recipe calls for kidney rather than pinto beans, and has another ingredient to add to the controversy— bourbon. A jigger added to Mom's chili during the last few minutes of simmerings produces a totally unexpected flavor. It's a great foil for the meat. As for the bourbon, there are those who might claim the addition of whiskey would dilute a good "bowl of red." Well, just serve them some and tell these "chili heads" it's the fastest way to enjoy their favorite food and drink! But it's important to simmer for no more than 5 or 10 minutes after adding the whiskey because it will quickly burn off. Also, since commercially canned kidney beans vary in sweetness and moisture, the liquid they're packed in should be tasted before adding it to the chili. If overly sweet, it's best to add plain water, juice from the canned tomatoes, or tomato juice. If the chili is too sweet, it will obscure the great whiskey flavor imparted by the bourbon.

All in all, this recipe produces a mild chili. If you like your chili a little "soupier," and want it to "bite back," add some Chili Gravy. Don't forget though: Add the bourbon last.

INGREDIENTS

1/4 cup olive oil

3 cloves garlic, thinly sliced

2 medium onions, diced

1 1/2 pounds lean ground chuck

3 cups canned crushed tomatoes

2 pounds home-cooked kidney beans, or 2 16-ounce cans, drained

1/2 teaspoon pepper

2 tablespoons chili powder

1/8 teaspoon ground cumin

1/8 teaspoon dried oregano

2 ounces bourbon
Salt to taste

METHOD

Heat the olive oil in a large skillet and sauté the garlic and onions until translucent. Remove the garlic and onions with a slotted spoon and set aside. Turn the heat to high and brown the meat in the skillet. Turn heat down, return the onions and garlic to the skillet, add the tomatoes, beans, and seasonings. Mix well. Bring to a simmer and simmer for 30 minutes. Add the bourbon; taste for seasonings, and add more if desired. Simmer for 5 minutes more and serve.

YIELD · 6—8 SERVINGS

UNC'S TEXAS RED

- 2 tablespoons lard, plus ¼ pound
- 3 tablespoons yellow cornmeal
- 1½ tablespoons masa harina or masa repa
- 1½ tablespoons ground cumin
- 1 tablespoon dried oregano
- 3 cloves garlic, minced
- 2 tablespoons mild ground chiles, or 3 tablespoons chili powder
- 1 quart beef stock or bouillon
- 3 tablespoons Gar's Chili Salsa (page 181)
- 3 pounds lean beef, cut into ¼"–½" cubes
- 4 cups chopped onions
- 1 28-ounce can crushed tomatoes (optional)
- Salt (see Note)

If there's happy Texas style, this is it. Nanny used to say, "Unc made our chili, and there was nothing in it but chili, no beans, just meat and chili." Well, this recipe does offer some tomatoes as an option —which in some parts of Texas is considered "adulteration." Either way, try it and see if this "bowl of red" doesn't make you smile.

METHOD

Heat 2 tablespoons lard in a skillet and sauté the cornmeal, masa, cumin, oregano, and garlic until golden brown. Add the ground chiles or chili powder and then the stock or bouillon, slowly stirring until the mixture is smooth and bubbly. Add the chili salsa. Set this "potion" aside.

In a large pot melt ¼ pound lard, then brown the beef in it, 1 pound at a time. Remove and set each batch aside until all the beef is browned. Sauté the onions in the fat left from browning until translucent. Return the beef to the pot. Then, slowly add the chili "potion," stirring until the mixture is once again smooth and bubbly. Add the tomatoes, if you insist. Salt to taste, if desired. Reduce to a simmer and cover. Let cook for 2 hours, skimming fat as necessary. If too thick add water.

NOTE: *Since commercially packaged chili powder and bouillon vary greatly in salt content, taste your chili first; you may not need any additional salt.*

YIELD · 6–8 SERVINGS

SON OF A GUN STEW— "THE CHILI OF CHAMPIONS"

"Son of a Gun Stew" can mean just about anything in the Lone Star State, and it doesn't always relate to food. "Rich as . . ." or "More full of . . ." . . . the possibilities are just as varied and equally questionable. Some say it's a stew of heart, lungs, and other organs, you name it. Others claim it's what the cowboys called what the cook couldn't identify. Everyone has his or her own idea about Son of a Gun Stew; this one's mine. If you like chili and you like to sweat from your eyebrows, you know what to call it. If you don't, you know what to call the cook!

METHOD

In a skillet melt 2 tablespoons lard, then sauté the masa, cornmeal, garlic, cumin, and oregano until golden brown. Add the ground chiles or chili powder and then the broth or bouillon, slowly stirring until the mixture is smooth and bubbly. Mix in the chili salsa thoroughly and set aside.

In a separate pot or Dutch oven, melt ¼ pound lard. Sauté the onions (and optional green pepper) until translucent; remove. Brown the meat in several batches, setting them aside as they brown. Return the meat and onions to the pot. Skim off any excess fat, and add the tomatoes. Slowly add the chili "potion," stirring until the mixture is once again smooth and bubbly. Salt to taste. Cover and simmer for 1½ hours. Add the beer and simmer, covered, for 20 to 30 minutes more before serving.

NOTE: *Since commercially packaged chili powder and bouillon vary greatly in salt content, taste your stew before adding salt; you may not need any.*

YIELD · 6–8 SERVINGS

INGREDIENTS

- 2 tablespoons lard, plus ¼ pound
- 1½ tablespoons masa harina or masa repa
- 1 tablespoon cornmeal
- 3 cloves garlic, minced
- 1½ tablespoons ground cumin
- 2 tablespoons dried oregano
- 3 tablespoons mild ground chiles, or 2 tablespoons chili powder
- 1½ quarts beef broth or bouillon
- 3 tablespoons Gar's Chili Salsa (page 181)
- 3 cups chopped onions
- 1½ pounds lean beef, cut into ¼"–½" cubes
- 1½ pounds lean venison or pork, cut into ¼"–½" cubes
- 1 28-ounce can crushed tomatoes
  Salt (see Note)
- ⅔ cup lager beer

OPTIONAL:
- 1 green bell pepper, seeded and chopped in ¼" dice

VENISON CHILI

No collection of chili recipes would be complete without at least one that features venison; devotees swear it has almost magical qualities that makes the flavor of chili spices "pop" like no other meat. Some "chiliheads" covet venison for its lean meat and faintly sweet, gamy flavor. They all seem to agree, though, that chili is one of the best uses for ground venison.

Since venison is so lean, it can easily cook up dry and mealy. The result makes the chili sauce seem almost watery. This recipe fights this problem, though, with a milder version of Nanny's Chili Gravy to let those special qualities of venison come through clearly.

INGREDIENTS

3 tablespoons lard

2 pounds ground or cubed venison

2 cloves garlic, minced

1 1/2 tablespoons masa harina or masa repa

1 tablespoon yellow cornmeal

1/2 teaspoon ground cumin

1/2 teaspoon dried oregano

3 tablespoons ground chiles

1 cup water

1 cup chopped canned plum tomatoes

1 cup chopped onions

1 cup mild picante salsa (available commercially)

1/2 cup beer

METHOD

In a large skillet melt 2 tablespoons lard and sauté the venison and garlic over medium-high heat, stirring, until the meat is browned. Remove the meat from the skillet with a slotted spoon.

Add the remaining tablespoon of lard to the pan, and sauté the masa, cornmeal, cumin, and oregano until golden brown. Gradually stir in the ground chiles and water and cook over low heat, stirring, until smooth and bubbly. Add the tomatoes, onions, and picante salsa and blend well. Return the meat to the pan and stir in the beer; blend well. Bring to a simmer and simmer, covered, for 30 minutes if you have used ground venison; if you have used cubed venison bake, covered, at 350°F for up to an hour.

YIELD · 6–8 SERVINGS

GUACAMOLE

The secrets to this classic Mexican salsa are several. First, freshly squeezed lime juice and a healthy dose of cumin bring out the best in really ripe avocados. Then, mashing the avocado to just the right consistency enhances the contrast between the diced tomatoes and onions. Finally, torching the guacamole with some of Gar's Chili Salsa or finely minced jalapeño pepper is like adding sparklers to a birthday cake.

The uses of guacamole go far beyond a dip. Adding guacamole to a lime juice vinaigrette makes a piquant salad dressing. It's also a terrific garnish for Huevos Rancheros, enchiladas, or omelettes. If you want to take it far and away from the Ranch, try a guacamole sandwich made with crusty black bread.

METHOD

In a bowl mash the avocados until the consistency of lumpy, coarsely mashed potatoes. Add the oil, lime juice, and spices. Blend well. Stir in the chopped tomato and onion and optional jalapeños or salsa. Cover tightly with plastic wrap and let stand for at least an hour to blend the flavors. Taste the guacamole; add more ground cumin if you like it more pungent.

YIELD · 2 ½ CUPS

INGREDIENTS

2–3 ripe California avocados, peeled

1 teaspoon pressed garlic

1 tablespoon olive oil

2 tablespoons freshly squeezed lime juice

1 teaspoon ground cumin or to taste

1 teaspoon salt

1/2 teaspoon pepper

1 medium tomato, peeled, seeded, and chopped into 3/8" dice

3 tablespoons red onion, chopped into 1/4" dice

OPTIONAL:

1–2 teaspoons chopped, seeded jalapeño pepper or

1/2 tablespoon Gar's Chili Salsa (page 181)

HUEVOS RANCHEROS

INGREDIENTS

Vegetable oil for
frying

4 corn tortillas

1 1/3 cup frijoles
(cooked pinto
beans, available
commercially)

1/3 cup chopped
canned mild
chiles, or
1 tablespoon
chopped seeded
fresh jalapeños

4 eggs

Lard or bacon
drippings
(optional) (1/2
tablespoon per
egg)

1 cup hot Chili
Gravy
(page 134)

1 teaspoon Gar's
Chili Salsa
(page 181)
(optional)

Served with Ranch-Style Guacamole, these
Tex-Mex eggs make a terrific brunch. The
beefy Chili Gravy ladled over the eggs and frijoles
perched on a freshly fried corn tortilla just tie it all
together. Add a couple of drops of Gar's Chili Salsa and
you may think you've died and gone to the "Last
Round-Up."

METHOD

In a skillet pour the oil 1″ deep and heat to 375°F. Fry the
tortillas until lightly browned and drain on paper towels.
Keep warm. Pour the oil from the pan and save for other
frying.

Add the frijoles and chopped chiles to the pan, mix well,
and sauté over low heat until a crust forms on the bottom.
Flip over and sauté until a second crust forms. Divide the
frijoles and place on the tortillas.

Poach the eggs or fry them in a pan in lard or bacon
drippings. Place 1 egg on each tortilla topped with the refried beans. Spoon 1/4 cup hot chili gravy over each egg and
garnish the top with 1/4 teaspoon (or to taste) salsa. This stuff
is *hot!* Serve immediately.

YIELD · 4 SERVINGS

NANNY'S ENCHILADA STACK

Most enchiladas are formed like crepes or manicotti by wrapping the tortillas around the filling. At the Ranch, popular Tex-Mex dinners often featured "stacks" of enchiladas. Tortillas were left flat and the filling and sauce were spread between layers to be served like individual cakes.

Nanny's Enchilada Stack is a real family favorite at the Ranch and is often served as the centerpiece of simple summer suppers. True to form, Nanny's method is quick and streamlined. Chili Gravy is ladled over quick-fried corn tortillas and then sprinkled with shredded cheese and chopped onions.

Repeated for 3 layers, the stacks are baked for 15 to 20 minutes and served when hot and bubbly—that's it! If you have some Chili Gravy on hand, these stacks can be made from start to finish in less than an hour. If not, add another 30 minutes to rustle up the gravy.

INGREDIENTS

Vegetable oil for frying

12 *tortillas*

2 *cups Chili Gravy (page 134)*

10 *ounces sharp Cheddar cheese, shredded*

1 *cup chopped scallions or spring onions*

METHOD

Preheat the oven to 350°F.

In a skillet pour the oil 1″ deep and heat to 375°F. Fry the tortillas until lightly browned and drain on paper towels.

Place 4 tortillas side by side in a baking dish or casserole. Ladle about 2 tablespoons chili gravy over each tortilla. Sprinkle one-third of the cheese over the tortillas. Sprinkle one-third of the onions over the cheese. Repeat twice more, with tortillas, gravy, cheese, and onions, making 4 stacks of 3 layers in all. Drizzle the remaining gravy evenly over the stacks, and place the pan in the oven for 15 to 20 minutes, until the cheese melts and the sauce is bubbly. Serve immediately.

YIELD · 4 SERVINGS

ENCHILADAS CON QUESO

Vegetable oil for frying

8 *corn tortillas*

2 *cups Chili Gravy (page 134)*

2 *cups shredded Monterey Jack cheese*

2 *4-ounce cans chopped mild chiles (or hot, to taste)*

1 *cup shredded sharp Cheddar cheese*

½ *cup chopped onion*

½ *cup sour cream*

This recipe is just a little fancier than Nanny's Enchilada Stack. It take a little longer to prepare, but you can make it a couple of hours ahead and bake it later. So, for eye appeal and convenience, these enchiladas are great party food.

For a different treat, try filling the tortillas with chili (less most of its juices) or diced chicken. For chicken, mix with just enough Cream Gravy to moisten it like tuna salad, and add some diced pimiento, if you like. The jalapeños are optional for either version.

METHOD

Preheat the oven to 350°F.

In a skillet pour the oil to a shallow level and heat. Sauté the tortillas quickly; they should remain soft. Drain the tortillas on paper towels.

Spread a little of the chili gravy in a baking dish just large enough to hold the tortillas when filled and rolled. Spread each tortilla with about 1 tablespoon of the chili gravy and then with ¼ cup Monterey Jack. Sprinkle about 1 tablespoon chopped chiles down the center of each tortilla. Fold 1 side of the tortilla over the chiles, then fold the other side over the first, as in folding a crepe or an omelette. Place the filled tortillas, folded sides down, in the baking dish. Spoon the rest of the chili gravy evenly over the enchiladas. Sprinkle a strip of Cheddar cheese and chopped onion down the center of each enchilada.

Bake for 10 to 15 minutes, until the cheese is melted and the sauce bubbles around the edges. Serve hot, garnished with sour cream.

YIELD · 4 SERVINGS

REFRITOS

From huevos rancheros to nachos, from breakfast to supper, there's always a place for refritos, or refried beans, in every Tex-Mex meal. The soaking and simmering take a while, but the beans refrigerate well and easily beat any that ever came out of a can.

METHOD

In a pot soak the beans in the water overnight.

Measure the beans and enough water to make 2 quarts including the beans and place in a large saucepan. Add the salt and half the garlic. Bring to the boil and boil for 10 minutes. Lower heat, cover, and simmer the beans 2 hours, or until tender. Drain the liquid from the beans and save.

Heat the lard or drippings in a large skillet and sauté the remaining garlic and the onion until translucent. If desired, add the oregano, cumin and/or jalapeño with the garlic and onion. Add the beans and mash with a wooden spoon or potato masher until well mashed and creamy, adding a little of the bean water if necessary. Fry over low heat until a crust forms; flip over and fry on the other side until a crust forms. Remove from the pan and keep warm until ready to use.

NOTE: *If necessary, continue to flip every couple of minutes until a thin crust forms. The time it takes will vary depending on the moisture content of the cooked beans. Also, if the frijoles are left to cook too long on one side, they will stick and eventually burn. It's best to move them around in the pan a bit. Add a little oil if necessary.*

YIELD · 4—6 SERVINGS

INGREDIENTS

- *1 pound pinto beans, rinsed and sorted*
- *3 quarts water*
- *1 tablespoon salt*
- *2 cloves garlic, minced*
- *3 tablespoons lard or bacon drippings*
- *1 small onion, chopped*

OPTIONAL:

- *3/4 teaspoon dried oregano (preferably Mexican), plus*
- *1/8 teaspoon cumin; and/or*
- *1 large fresh jalapeño, finely chopped*

SOPAIPILLAS

INGREDIENTS

1½ cups all-purpose
   flour

 2 teaspoons baking
   powder

½ teaspoon salt

 4 tablespoons solid
   vegetable
   shortening

½ cup milk
   Vegetable oil for
   frying

Tex-Mex dinners just aren't quite the same without these light and airy treats. Nanny called them "fried pies" in a recipe which—true to form —turned up on the back of an envelope. They're as light and crisp as any I've had anywhere. Sopaipillas are traditionally eaten by tearing off a corner and drizzling a little honey inside. For variety, try some of Nanny's Plum Jelly in place of the honey.

METHOD

In a bowl mix the flour, baking powder, and salt. Cut in the shortening until the mixture resembles coarse meal. Stir in the milk to make a soft dough. Add a little more milk if the dough is too dry. Knead the dough gently until smooth and soft. Cover with plastic wrap and let sit for 10 to 15 minutes.

In a deep pan or fryer pour the oil 2″ deep and heat to 400°F.

Roll the dough out on a floured board until ⅛″ thick. Cut into squares or triangles about 4″ on a side. Slide a square into the hot fat and hold it under the surface of the oil, using a spatula or a slotted spoon. In about 10 seconds, the square will strain to come to the surface and will begin to puff. When it puffs, let it come to the surface and brown lightly for a few seconds, then turn it over and let the other side brown. Remove the square and drain on paper towels. Keep warm. Repeat with the remaining squares, but be sure to reheat the oil to 400° each time.

Serve hot, or reheat in a 350° oven for 5 minutes. (Leftover dough scraps will not puff.) Serve with jelly or honey.

YIELD · 6–8 SOPAIPILLAS

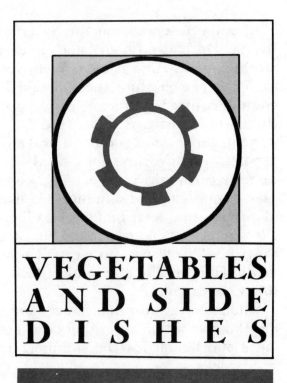

VEGETABLES AND SIDE DISHES

Over the years, the variety of fruits and vegetables grown at the Ranch has only been outdone by the cast of characters who raised them. During Nanny's sixty-five years as matriarch of the Houghton Ranch, the number of farmhands that came and went ran into the hundreds. Some even became part of the lore and legends that surround the Ranch. Fact or fiction, though, recollections of them certainly made good "dinner talk."

Right at the top of the list was Rube Willis, foreman. An expert cowboy and farmer, he also had a way with engines like some people have with animals. When I knew him, Rube was well into his seventies and still going strong. He had no teeth, and he carried his dentures around in his shirt pocket. Well, you couldn't always understand everything the man said, but apparently the engines could. If a tractor or pump wouldn't start, old Rube would just cuss at it till it did.

Next, there was a gentle soul called William, who was a particular favorite of us children. He loved to sit under a great apricot tree at night and tell us stories or play a good game of dominoes. William was almost out of another era, wearing blue Headlight brand bib overalls, khaki work shirts rolled up at the sleeve, and a dusty black twill snap-brim cap. To watch him work the fields with his favorite mule, Ruby, was a flashback thirty or forty years.

Others were more like Lars. Lars came down from the Dakotas with a threshing crew and decided to stay on at the Ranch for the summer. Tall and lanky, of

UNC AT
THE
CONTROLS
OF A ONE-
HORSE
MOWING
MACHINE

Norwegian stock, he talked with an incredibly slow, nasal drawl and wore a baseball cap pushed up at the brim. As farmhands go, Lars had a strong back, and could pick low-growing black-eyed peas for hours without straightening up. What struck us about Lars, though, was his teen-age wife, Thelma, who was a good twenty years his junior. He "found" her in the Ozarks living in a shack crammed with other children and no electricity or indoor plumbing. Before he brought her to the Ranch, in the early sixties, Thelma had never even seen a vacuum cleaner!

Then there were "sports" like Gus. Gus was Mexican, and as Nanny put it, "a good man with a hoe." He was even better with trotlines and was always running up to the lakes to check them. The catfish Gus pulled out of the lakes were huge. Some had heads the size of cantaloupes, and were real trophies. To show off his catch, he'd mount their heads on the trunk of a cottonwood next to the door of his quarters.

One day Gus said he didn't feel well, and stayed in his bunk. Come noon, however, he showed up for dinner. Nanny had a cup of weak tea set at his place. No sugar, lemon, or milk, just weak tea. No plate, silverware, nothing. "What's this?" Gus wanted to know. "Well," Nanny snapped, "if you don't feel well, you can't be hungry!"

Shorty, on the other hand, didn't do too much in the fields, but he can't be left out. Nanny would pick him up in Amarillo, and he would insist on riding in the cargo space of her station wagon for the hour and a half ride to the Ranch. On arrival and without explanation, he sometimes just turned around and walked back!

His greatest accomplishment was achieved the day he decided to stay and work. When they got to the Ranch, he headed for his quarters across the creek—over a railroad-tie "footbridge" that spans this three-foot-wide, six-inch-deep stream just above the water. Well, Shorty must have had too much to drink because he didn't

make it. We've never been able to figure out how he did it, but he fell off the bridge and into the creek head first!

When it came to the gardens, it's clear that Nanny had a few fruitcakes baking in the sun as well as in the oven. The funny stories weren't confined to the hands, either. We've howled more than once over the time someone sent Unc a thirty-five-pound watermelon, express collect. Unc was so mad he went out to the melon patch, picked six big ones, and sent them back the same way!

Of course, the melons weren't missed. There were dozens more in the patch just like them. The orchards and gardens provided a veritable cornucopia. So, thanks to the help of these folk, and many more like them, Martha Houghton had the freshest ingredients to cook with.

When it came to vegetables, she clearly favored corn, tomatoes, eggplant, and squash. Onions, it seems, were used as often as black pepper—an important ingredient for adding a sweet, spicy edge to dishes that frequently traced their roots to the deep South.

The balance of these recipes are a good representation of what was served fresh from the garden.

STEPPING ONTO ''THE HURRICANE DECK'': BREAKING HORSES AT THE HOUGHTON RANCH, ABOUT 1915

VEGETABLE DISHES

RANCH BEANS

1 pound pinto beans

3 quarts water

1½ tablespoons chili powder, or to taste

⅛ pound salt pork, cut into ½" cubes

Salt to taste

These beans are just like the kind they serve at the "free feed" barbecue at the XIT Rodeo & Reunion held in Dalhart, Texas (hometown to the Ranch some forty miles away). The recipe presented here makes about eight servings, a little less than most recipes that made it to Nanny's Texas table—and a lot less than the recipe used to serve the 20,000 people who attend the Rodeo. (It calls for 800 pounds of beans!)

These beans keep and reheat quite well. They're also very handy for making up a quick batch of Refritos. Be sure to save some of the liquid from cooking the beans. If they become too dry when reheating or frying, just add the liquid as needed.

METHOD

In a pot, soak the beans in the water overnight.

Over low heat bring to a simmer, add the chili powder and salt pork, and simmer, uncovered, for 2½ to 3 hours, or until the beans are tender and the liquid has thickened. Add more boiling water, if necessary, during the cooking to keep the beans just covered. Toward the end of the cooking time, taste carefully for seasoning and add salt to taste.

YIELD · ABOUT 8 SERVINGS

GREEN BEANS

This is a slightly lighter version of an old Ranch favorite. The beans are cooked in less time and less bacon fat—they're still smoky and sweet with onion, but are crisper, greener, and less greasy. Though these beans are not just like Nanny used to make, it's safe to suggest that this is the way she would make them if she were with us today. She was very well read and intensely interested in good nutrition. So, it's likely she would have adopted this healthier, more modern approach to cooking vegetables.

INGREDIENTS

3 cups water

1 pound green beans, washed, trimmed, and cut into 1" pieces

1/4 pound chunk bacon, cut into 1/2" cubes

1/2 teaspoon pepper

1 medium onion, quartered

Salt to taste

METHOD

In a saucepan bring the water to a boil; add the beans, bacon, and pepper. Place the onion quarters on top. Boil, partially covered, for 5 minutes, lower heat, and simmer, covered, for another 15 minutes. Remove the onion, drain, correct the seasoning with salt, and serve immediately.

YIELD · 4 SERVINGS

BAKED LIMA BEANS

No chuck wagon ever left the Headquarters without full rations of bacon, onions, and dried beans—the prime ingredients in this hearty dish. The sauce around the limas in this recipe by a Fort Worth relative, the late Mrs. Walter Caldwell, is pleasantly creamy and spiked with onion. Good with any pungent meat, the beans get better if made a day in advance and reheated. In other words, allow 2 days in all to make this recipe.

This recipe is reprinted from the 1928 *Woman's Club of Fort Worth Cookbook*.

INGREDIENTS

- 1 1/2 cups dried lima beans
- 1/4 pound bacon, cut into 1" pieces
- 2 medium onions, sliced
- 1/2 teaspoon salt
- 1/2 teaspoon pepper
- 1 cup milk

METHOD

In a pot soak the beans in water overnight. The next day, boil until soft and drain.

In a hot skillet fry the bacon until cooked but not crisp. Remove the bacon, lower heat, and sauté the onions in the bacon drippings until soft.

Preheat the oven to 350°F. Grease a casserole.

Put a layer of beans in the casserole. Top with some of the onion and bacon, salt, and pepper. Repeat the layers until all the ingredients are used. Pour the milk over all and bake for 30 minutes, until golden brown on top.

NOTE: *For a thicker sauce, try a standard white sauce in place of the milk. Or, better yet, try Nanny's Cheddar Cheese Sauce (page 178).*

YIELD · 4 SERVINGS

HARVARD-STYLE BEETS

Most recipes for Harvard beets call for a few cloves and a thick, tart sauce. This version features onion in place of the cloves and less vinegar and cornstarch. The result is less imposing and sticky-sweet. They taste a little more "fresh from the garden." Nanny frequently served them with Ranch Fried Steak, but they're also very good with duck, venison, or antelope.

METHOD

Place the beets in a large saucepan and cover with water. Bring to a boil and cover; cook until tender, 20 to 30 minutes. Remove the beets with a slotted spoon and let them cool. Reserve the cooking water.

When cool enough to handle, peel the beets and slice them into ⅛" slices. Ladle out 1⅔ cups of the beet water and save. Discard the rest, including any sand in the bottom of the pan. Rinse the pan out and return the reserved beet water to it. Add the vinegar, sugar, onion, salt, and pepper and heat until the sugar dissolves. Add the cornstarch mixture, and simmer, stirring, until the sauce is smooth and thickened. Return the beets to the pan and stir gently to coat the beets and heat through.

YIELD · 4 SERVINGS

INGREDIENTS

- 2 pounds beets, washed
- ⅓ cup cider vinegar
- ½ cup sugar
- 1 small onion, diced
- ½ teaspoon salt
- ½ teaspoon pepper
- 1 tablespoon cornstarch dissolved in 2 tablespoons cold water

GLAZED CARROTS

*1 pound carrots,
    peeled and cut into
    2¹/2"-x-¹/4" sticks*

2 tablespoons butter

1 teaspoon sugar

¹/2 teaspoon salt

¹/4 teaspoon pepper

*Jalapeño Salsa Jelly
(optional)
(page 231)*

 Even if I did pass my share on to other "lucky" recipients, I can at least recall that these glazed carrots—as simple as they are—were enjoyed by many.

METHOD

In a saucepan put the carrot sticks and enough water to just cover and boil until barely tender, 8 to 10 minutes. Add the butter, sugar, salt, and pepper to the carrots, mixing well, and heat until glazed.

If desired, substitute one or more teaspoons to taste of the salsa jelly for the sugar to make "caliente" carrots.

YIELD · 4 SERVINGS

CORN FRITTERS

*Vegetable oil for
frying*

2 eggs, separated

*1 cup all-purpose
    flour*

*³/4 teaspoon baking
    powder*

³/4 teaspoon salt

¹/2 cup milk

*1 cup cooked fresh,
    canned, or defrosted
    corn kernels*

For breakfast, with lots of syrup and crisp bacon, there's nothing quite like these corn fritters. Served without syrup, they're also quite nice with ham, roast pork, or broiled fish. Nanny's version cook up like little pan beignets or fluffy doughnuts. If you can't use all the fritters at once, they can be refrigerated for up to a week or frozen for up to 3 months without losing their flavor.

METHOD

Pour the vegetable oil 2" deep in a fryer or deep skillet; heat to 375°F.

Beat the egg yolks until lemon-colored. In a bowl blend the flour, baking powder, and salt. Stir in the yolks, milk and 1 teaspoon oil until well blended. Beat the egg whites until frothy and gently fold into the batter. Then fold in the corn.

Deep-fry by big spoonfuls (about 2 tablespoonsful or 2″) for 5 minutes, turning once. Fry a few fritters at a time, and reheat the oil to 375° between batches. Drain on paper towels and serve hot.

YIELD · ABOUT 16 FRITTERS

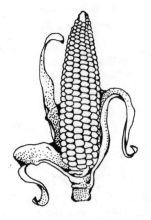

CORN PUDDING

One of Nanny's best-loved recipes for corn is this onion-flecked custard casserole. It makes a great sidekick for fried or broiled fish. For years, we've enjoyed Corn Pudding back East with freshly caught Pan-Fried Trout.

METHOD

Preheat the oven to 350°F. Butter a 7″ baking dish.

Melt 1 tablespoon butter in a small skillet and sauté the onion in it. Set aside.

Melt the remaining tablespoon butter in a saucepan and stir in the flour. Pour in the milk gradually, stirring until smooth. Bring the mixture to the boil, stirring frequently. When thickened and smooth, add the corn, sautéed onion, salt, pepper, sugar, and eggs, beaten until light and foamy. Mix well. Pour into the prepared dish and bake for 35 to 40 minutes, until lightly browned.

YIELD · 4 SERVINGS

INGREDIENTS

2 *tablespoons butter*

¼ *cup chopped onion*

2 *tablespoons flour*

1 *cup milk*

1 *cup fresh, canned, or defrosted corn kernels*

1½ *teaspoons salt*

¼ *teaspoon pepper*

1½ *teaspoons sugar*

2 *eggs*

CORN SOUFFLÉ

Martha Houghton's Corn Soufflé, adapted from a recipe found in her well-used copy of *The Five O'Clock Tea Club Cookbook,* is the most delicate way to enjoy corn I know—on the cob or off. Diced fresh jalapeños add a lively touch that makes this dish terrific with glazed ham or cold, sliced tenderloin. For an elegant buffet, serve this corn soufflé with either of these meats, salad, and biscuits. Nanny's Frozen Mocha Cheesecake or Almond-Coconut Snow Cake are good ways to top it off.

INGREDIENTS

- *1 tablespoon butter*
- *2 tablespoons flour*
- *1 cup milk*
- *1 cup fresh, canned, or defrosted corn kernels*
- *1 green jalapeño pepper, seeded and minced*
- *½ teaspoon salt*
- *¼ teaspoon pepper*
- *1 teaspoon sugar*
- *2 eggs, separated*

METHOD

Preheat the oven to 350°F. Butter a 7" 1½-quart soufflé dish.

In a saucepan melt the butter. Stir in the flour. Pour in the milk gradually, stirring until smooth. Bring the mixture to the boil, stirring frequently. When thickened and smooth, add the corn, jalapeño, salt, pepper, and sugar. Beat the egg yolks until thick and lemon-colored and add to the saucepan.

Let the mixture cool while beating the egg whites until stiff. Fold the whites into the corn mixture and pour into the prepared dish. Bake for 30 to 35 minutes, until puffed and browned.

YIELD · 4 SERVINGS

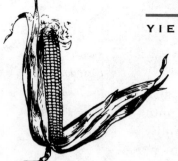

EGGPLANT CASSEROLE

At the Ranch, eggplant and corn ripen at about the same time, so they are occasionally teamed to produce this colorful casserole. The aggressive additions of black pepper and onion wake up the flavor in the milder corn and eggplant, making this dish terrific company for ham or pork.

M E T H O D

Place the eggplant in a medium-size bowl, add the 2 tablespoons salt and enough water to cover and let soak for 1 hour. Drain and pat dry. Butter a 3-quart baking dish.

Preheat the oven to 375°F.

Place the eggplant in the baking dish, cover with the onion, then the green pepper, then the corn. Add ½ teaspoon salt, pepper, and celery seed, then top with the bread crumbs. Pour the chicken broth over the bread crumbs, then drizzle on the melted butter. Bake for 1 hour, until golden brown and crusty on top.

YIELD · 4–6 SERVINGS

I N G R E D I E N T S

- *1 large eggplant, peeled and cut into 1" cubes*
- *2 tablespoons salt, plus ½ teaspoon*
- *1 onion, minced*
- *1 green pepper, minced*
- *2 cups fresh, canned, or defrosted corn kernels*
- *½ teaspoon pepper*
- *⅛ teaspoon celery seed*
- *2 cups dried bread crumbs*
- *1 cup chicken broth*
- *2 tablespoons butter, melted*

EGGPLANT FRITTERS

Nanny used to coax wary children into trying these delectable discs by saying "they were Unc's favorite." I had to be urged just once. The coating is crunchy and the fritters just thick enough to make the eggplant cook up creamy and release its eggy, buttery aroma. You can can use cracker meal, but finely ground fresh saltines will produce a much more interesting crust.

INGREDIENTS

1 1-pound
   eggplant, washed
   and sliced into
   1/4"–1/2"-thick
   rounds

   Salt and pepper

   Vegetable oil for
   frying

1/2 cup all-purpose
   flour

2 eggs

4–6 ounces saltines
   (about 40–60
   crackers)

METHOD

Spread the eggplant slices on a plate, salt lightly, turn the slices over, and salt lightly again. Place another plate on the slices and weight it down. Let the slices sit for at least an hour. Drain off the liquid and pat the slices dry.

Pour the vegetable oil 2" deep in a fryer or deep skillet; heat to 375°F.

Place the flour in a shallow bowl and lightly season with salt and pepper. Place the eggs in a separate shallow bowl and beat lightly. Grind the saltines to fine crumbs in a food processor or put them in a plastic bag and crush with a rolling pin. Place the crumbs in another shallow bowl.

Dredge the eggplant slices lightly in the flour, dip in the eggs and dredge in the crumbs, patting with a metal spatula or flat blade of a knife so crumbs adhere. Deep-fry a few at a time about 1 minute on each side. Drain on paper towels. Be sure to reheat the oil to 375° for every batch. Serve hot.

YIELD · 3–4 SERVINGS

CREOLE-STUFFED EGGPLANT

Martha Houghton loved eggplant and was fond of serving it in all kinds of ways. This recipe, found in the 1928 *Woman's Club of Fort Worth Cookbook*, produces a fiery ratatouille festively presented in the eggplant's own shell.

METHOD

Preheat the oven to 325°F. Butter a baking dish.

In a pot of water boil the eggplant whole for 10 to 15 minutes. Cut in half. Using a grapefruit knife, remove the pulp to within 1/2" of the skin, being careful not to pierce the skin. Chop the pulp.

INGREDIENTS

2 small or 1 large
   eggplant

4 tablespoons butter

1 onion, chopped

1 small garlic clove,
   minced

1 large green pepper,
   seeded, deveined,
   and chopped

   (continued)

In a large frying pan melt 3 tablespoons butter. Add the pulp, onion, garlic, and green pepper. Cook for 5 minutes without browning. Remove the pan from the heat and stir in the tomatoes, eggs, bay leaf, salt, and pepper. Stuff the shells and place in the baking dish.

Combine the bread crumbs with the remaining tablespoon of butter and sprinkle over the eggplant shells. Bake for 1 hour, until browned.

YIELD · 4–6 SERVINGS

3 medium tomatoes, peeled, seeded, and chopped

3 eggs, hard-cooked and finely chopped

1/8 teaspoon powdered bay leaf

1/4 teaspoon salt

1/2 teaspoon pepper

1 cup bread crumbs

OKRA CREOLE

Martha Houghton was quite fond of okra and loved recipes that gave this bland, southern pod a bit of sting. She particularly liked this one which came from her friend Velma Craig of Amarillo. Okra is lightly stewed with tomatoes, bacon, and onion and then stung (or given the proportions, you might say "torched") with pepper and Tabasco.

INGREDIENTS

4 strips bacon

1 large onion, chopped

1 pound small okra pods, washed

1 large tomato, peeled, and cut into eighths

1 teaspoon brown sugar

1/2 teaspoon salt

1/2 teaspoon pepper

1/2–1 teaspoon Tabasco sauce

M E T H O D

In a skillet fry the bacon until crisp and set aside on paper towels to drain.

Sauté the onion in the bacon fat. Add the okra and tomatoes and cook until tender but not soft, 7 to 10 minutes. Add the brown sugar and salt, then add the pepper and Tabasco (start with the smaller amount of Tabasco, and then add according to taste). Stir. Turn off the heat and cover with a lid to steam slightly. Serve hot.

YIELD · 4 SERVINGS

STEAMED OKRA

INGREDIENTS

*1 pound okra, washed
and trimmed to the
caps of the pods*

*2 tablespoons butter
Cayenne or white
pepper to taste*

This was Martha Houghton's favorite way to make okra. It's mine, too. Her generation cooked their vegetables until completely soft and, unfortunately, they lost most of their nutritive value. Therefore, to bring this recipe up to date, the cooking time has been shortened considerably. The result is okra that's pleasantly crunchy with a nutty, string bean–like flavor. Cooked this way, the okra also turns a pleasant, bright green and the usual "roping" or sliminess is cut to a minimum. At the Ranch, we sprinkle a few drops of vinegar flavored with Tabasco sauce on the okra just before eating. It's a delicious example of how South meets West in Nanny's cooking!

METHOD

In a pot bring enough salted water to just cover the pods to the boil, add the okra, and boil, uncovered, until just tender and still bright green, 3 to 4 minutes. Drain. Dot with butter and sprinkle with cayenne or white pepper. Cover the pan and let stand for a few minutes. Gently stir to coat the okra well and serve hot.

YIELD · 3–4 SERVINGS

ONION PIE

 If you want to know what the onions grown at the Houghton Ranch taste like, try this recipe. Sliced small white onions are barely sautéed and then baked in a quichelike filling just long enough to give them the consistency of crème caramel. The result is mild, sweet, and crunchy. There are no tears to shed over the custard filling either! To achieve the delicate consistency of the filling around the onions, be sure not to overcook. To test for doneness, slide the pan back and forth on the oven rack; the filling should quiver just a little. Serve promptly—if it cools too long, the pie will lose its tender texture and become too solid.

INGREDIENTS

1 crust for a 9" pie

1 pound small white onions, about 1" to 1½" in diameter

2 tablespoons butter

3 eggs

1 cup heavy cream

1 cup milk

½ teaspoon salt

½ teaspoon pepper

METHOD

Preheat the oven to 400°F. Fit the crust into a 9" pieplate, line with buttered foil, fill with pie weights or beans, and bake for 10 minutes. Remove the weights and foil, prick the crust in a few places, and bake for 5 minutes more. Remove from the oven and let cool while preparing the filling, keeping the oven on.

Raise the oven temperature to 450°.

Bring a pot of water to the boil. Drop in the onions and simmer for 10 to 15 seconds. Drain the onions and peel; the skins should slip off very easily. Slice the onions into ¼" slices. Separate the slices into rings. Melt the butter in a skillet and sauté the rings for 2 minutes, until barely softened, but still round. Spread the rings evenly in the prepared piecrust.

In a bowl beat the eggs with the cream, milk, salt, and pepper until blended. Pour the mixture over the onion rings. Carefully place the pie in the oven, bake for 10 minutes, then reduce the oven heat to 300° and bake for 30 to 35 minutes more, until just set and a knife inserted in the center comes out clean. Serve hot or warm.

YIELD · 8 SERVINGS

BLACK-EYED PEAS

Whenever I think of dinner at the Ranch, I inevitably recall wonderful bowls of black-eyed peas simmered with ham hocks, their aroma smoky and kind of buttery-rich as the steam rose. Always served with beef or ham, they're a staple of which I have never tired. For a little more color or variety, you might try adding some chopped fresh parsley before serving; it makes for a nice contrast with the smoky-gray beans.

INGREDIENTS

½ pound dried black-eyed peas

3–4 cups water

½ teaspoon salt

½ teaspoon pepper

4 strips bacon, or ¼ pound ham, diced, or ½ pound ham hock

3–4 tablespoons butter

OPTIONAL:

Chopped fresh parsley

METHOD

In a pot soak the peas overnight in the water seasoned with the salt and pepper.

Bring the mixture to a simmer, add the bacon, ham, or ham hock, and simmer for 45 minutes, or until the peas are soft. Skim as necessary, and add boiling water, if necessary. When the peas are tender, drain any remaining water, add the butter, and check for seasonings, adding more salt and pepper to taste. Garnish with parsley, if desired.

YIELD · 4 SERVINGS

WILD RICE

Wild rice and wild game go together like meat and potatoes. Mallard and pintail duck, Canada geese, dove, and quail are particularly plentiful at the Houghton Ranch. So, needless to say, there are many occasions (in season) to serve wild rice. This version makes a crunchy, nutty rice that's a robust compliment to any wild fowl. To serve with venison, antelope, or other wild, red meat, substitute beef broth for chicken.

METHOD

Preheat the oven to 325°F.

Heat the oil in a frying pan and sauté the garlic and onion until limp. Add the parsley and wild rice and sauté over medium heat for 4 to 5 minutes, stirring frequently. Remove from heat, put the rice mixture into an ovenproof casserole, pour in the boiling water and stock, and salt to taste. Cover the dish, place in the oven, and bake for 15 minutes, then lower heat to 300° and bake for another 45 minutes or until tender. Serve hot.

YIELD · 4–6 SERVINGS

INGREDIENTS

- ¼ cup vegetable or olive oil
- 1 clove garlic, minced
- ½ cup finely chopped onion
- 3 tablespoons chopped fresh parsley
- 1 cup raw wild rice
- 1 cup boiling water
- 1 cup chicken or beef stock, boiling

  Salt to taste

SQUASH AU GRATIN

Next to tomatoes, no vegetable at the Houghton Ranch received more attention or inventive approaches than the common yellow summer squash. A row or two seemed to produce an almost endless supply well into early fall. This recipe, possibly adapted from a recipe on the side of a breadcrumb box, is especially suitable for squash that is picked young— at about 4 to 6 inches. It sets off the sweet taste and offers lots of eye appeal. Split lengthwise, the little squash boats are stuffed with toasted bread crumbs and cheese. Unlike most of Martha Houghton's squash recipes, this one contains no pepper, which allows the delicate contrast between the vegetable and stuffing to come through clearly. For variety, try other cheeses such as Parmesan or Gruyère. The change in taste can be subtle but worthwhile.

INGREDIENTS

- 6 medium summer squash, washed, stems trimmed
- 4 tablespoons butter
- 1 cup toasted bread crumbs
- ½ cup wheat germ
- ¼ pound Cheddar cheese (or Parmesan or Gruyère), shredded

METHOD

Place squash in a pan of boiling water and simmer for 10 to 15 minutes, until barely tender when pierced with a knife tip. Drain and cut lengthwise. Remove the seeds.

In a skillet melt the butter and stir in the bread crumbs and wheat germ.

Fill the cavities of the squash with the crumb mixture. Top with the cheese. Place under the broiler to brown and melt the cheese. (If you wish to prepare the squash in advance, bake in a 400°F oven for 15 minutes to brown and melt the cheese.)

YIELD · 6 SERVINGS

SQUASH PANCAKES

INGREDIENTS

- 2 cups mashed or riced cooked squash
- 3 tablespoons butter, melted
- 1 teaspoon minced fresh parsley
- 1 teaspoon salt
- 1/4 teaspoon pepper
- 1/4 teaspoon celery salt
- 1/4 teaspoon paprika
- 1/2 teaspoon onion juice
- 1 egg, beaten
- 1/2 cup sifted all-purpose flour
- 1/2 teaspoon baking powder
- 1/4–1/2 cup milk

Nanny received this "controversial" recipe from my mother Pauline Ross, who ultimately had it published in Neiman-Marcus's *A Taste of Texas* in 1949. This is only controversial in that Mother claims that she overheard me brag, at the age of 10, "My mother makes terrific squash pancakes." At the horrified expression of my playmate, I immediately changed my tone to, "but I hate 'em!" As for the controversy, I don't remember such blatant disloyalty, but obviously, someone does!

As for the pancakes, they're slightly sweet and thin, like Swedish pancakes, but predictably heavier due to the squash. Serve them with roast pork, fresh ham, or veal and they won't be controversial. However, be prepared for a loyal following.

METHOD

Be sure the squash is well drained. Mix thoroughly in a bowl with all the other ingredients, using only 1/4 cup milk if the squash is watery. The batter should be thick enough to drop by spoonfuls, but thin enough to spread.

Heat a lightly greased griddle and drop the batter, about
2 tablespoonfuls at a time, onto the griddle. Tip the griddle
slightly to spread the pancakes (they should be about 3½").
Cook about 2 minutes per side, turning once when the cakes
look slightly dry on top. Serve immediately.

YIELD · ABOUT 24 PANCAKES

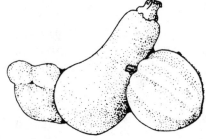

CREAMY SUMMER SQUASH

If I have waxed poetic about how this favorite
recipe was served in a beautiful old calico-blue
serving piece, it is not without reason. Nanny served
this dish often, and it was joyfully consumed even by
those who didn't care for squash of any kind.

Bright yellow summer squash and white onions are
slowly cooked down, drained of most of their water, and
then mashed fine. A healthy dose of pepper sets off the
buttery summer squash and sweet onion flavors. For an
even creamier version, stir in a couple of tablespoons of
sour cream just before serving.

INGREDIENTS

- 2 pounds summer
  squash, cut into
  ½" chunks
- 1 medium onion,
  diced
- ½ cup water
- 2 tablespoons butter
- 1 teaspoon salt
- ½ teaspoon pepper

OPTIONAL:

- 1 egg, hard-cooked
  and chopped
- 2–4 tablespoons sour
  cream

METHOD

In a frying pan bring the squash and onion to a simmer in
the water and butter. Cook the mixture, covered, until
tender, about 10 minutes. Remove the cover, boil off the
remaining water, and mash the mixture well with a wooden
spoon or potato masher. Drain off any liquid. Add the salt
and pepper.

If desired, garnish with the egg, or stir in the sour cream.
Serve hot.

YIELD · 4 SERVINGS

SQUASH SOUFFLÉ

The average squash recipe is quite solid or heavy due to the high percentage of water in this edible gourd. For a somewhat lighter change, this soufflé elevates the sweet, nutty flavor of squash a rung or two. This recipe is reprinted from the 1928 *Woman's Club of Fort Worth Cookbook.*

INGREDIENTS

- *3 pounds winter squash, peeled, seeded, and cut into 1" chunks*
- *1 cup water*
- *2 eggs, separated*
- *1 teaspoon onion juice or grated onion*
- *1½ tablespoons flour*
- *1 teaspoon Worcestershire sauce*
- *½ teaspoon salt*
- *¼ teaspoon pepper*

METHOD

Preheat the oven to 350°F. Butter a 2-quart baking dish.

Steam the squash on a rack set in a pot with 1 cup water 15 to 20 minutes or until tender. Puree in a food processor or food mill. There should be about 4 cups of squash.

Add the egg yolks, onion, flour, Worcestershire sauce, salt, and pepper to the squash. Beat the egg whites until stiff and fold into the squash mixture. Pour into the baking dish and bake for 45 to 50 minutes.

YIELD · 4–6 SERVINGS

FRENCH-FRIED SWEET POTATOES

Fried crisp like julienne or shoestring potatoes, these "French fries" are like peanuts—once you start eating them, it's hard to stop! Martha Houghton considered them a festive treat and sometimes served them with catfish—you might call this combination "Fish and Chips Houghton Ranch Style." For a change, try them with ribs.

M E T H O D

Heat the oil in a deep fryer (or in a frying pan with oil 1″ deep) to 375°F.

Fry the sweet potato sticks until cooked, 2 to 3 minutes. Remove from the oil and drain on absorbent paper. Reheat the oil and refry the potatoes for another 1 to 2 minutes to crisp up. Remove, drain on paper towels, sprinkle with salt and paprika, and serve hot.

YIELD · 2 SERVINGS

INGREDIENTS

Vegetable oil for frying

1 large sweet potato, peeled and cut into sticks

Salt

Paprika

SUCCOTASH

Even if you don't like limas, Nanny's version of succotash is worth a try. Creamy and well-seasoned with salt and pepper, it's great with Smothered Pork Chops or pot roast.

M E T H O D

Cook the beans and corn in separate pots until tender. Mix together, add the butter, salt, and pepper, and blend well. Stir in the cream, heat until hot, and serve immediately.

NOTE: *Don't try this with canned lima beans, which will make mushy, watery succotash.*

YIELD · 4 SERVINGS

INGREDIENTS

2 cups fresh baby lima beans, or 1 10-ounce frozen package

2 cups fresh corn kernels, or 1 10-ounce frozen package

1 tablespoon butter

1–1½ teaspoons salt

½ teaspoon pepper

½ cup heavy cream

FRIED TOMATOES

This is the original "can't wait, too late" recipe. Nanny would serve these delectable fritters early in the summer season before the tomatoes became fully ripe. She just couldn't wait. Then later, when it was "too late" for tomatoes to ripen, a good many green tomatoes went right from the vine to the pan. If you don't have red-ripe tomatoes, green tomatoes will do. Of course, they'll need to cook longer and slower than red ones. The flavor will be different, too, more like green peppers.

INGREDIENTS

4 tomatoes, washed
1 cup milk
1 cup finely crushed saltines mixed with ½ teaspoon pepper
3 tablespoons butter
3 tablespoons vegetable oil

METHOD

Trim a thin slice off the top and bottom of each tomato and discard. Cut the tomatoes into ½" slices. Dip the slices in the milk, then dredge in the cracker crumbs and pepper, patting the crumbs on with a spreader.

Melt a tablespoon butter with 1 tablespoon oil in a medium-size skillet. Sauté a few of the slices over medium to medium-high heat until golden brown, about 1 minute, then turn and sauté for 1 minute more, until golden brown. Remove to a heated platter. Add more butter and oil as needed, discarding any that has burned, and sauté the remaining slices. If frying green tomatoes, use low to medium heat and cook until tender. Serve hot.

YIELD · 4 SERVINGS

GRILLED TOMATOES

Tomatoes made it to Nanny's table in every conceivable fashion—in soups, salads, stews, sauces, and as a major ingredient in any number of casseroles. This recipe is a fine example; it's based on something clipped from an unidentified magazine which presents red, ripe tomatoes at their best. The brown sugar brings out their sweet, tangy nature and Nanny's cheese sauce makes a nice, sharp foil. They're particularly good served with beef or rich, gamy meat.

INGREDIENTS

3 large, firm tomatoes, washed

1 egg, beaten

1/3 cup fine dry bread crumbs mixed with 1/2 teaspoon salt and 1/8 teaspoon pepper

2 tablespoons butter, melted, plus 1 tablespoon, unmelted

2 tablespoons brown sugar

Cheese Sauce (optional) (recipe below)

METHOD

Remove a thin slice from the top and bottom of each tomato. Cut in half, making 2 thick slices of each tomato. Dip each slice in the beaten egg and then in the bread crumbs mixed with the salt and pepper. Place, smaller end up, on a rack in a broiling pan and drizzle 1/2 teaspoon butter on each.

Broil, 7" to 8" from the heat, for 6 minutes. Turn the slices over, drizzle the remaining melted butter on each, and broil for another 6 minutes. Top each slice with a teaspoon brown sugar, dot with the unmelted butter, and broil for another 2 to 3 minutes, until crusty. Serve immediately, passing the cheese sauce on the side, if desired.

YIELD · 6 SERVINGS

Cheese Sauce

In a saucepan melt the butter, stir in flour, and when smooth, add the milk. Bring to a simmer and simmer until thick and smooth. Add the salt and stir in the Cheddar. When the cheese is melted and smooth, remove the sauce from heat and serve immediately.

1 tablespoon butter

1 tablespoon flour

1 cup milk

1/2 teaspoon salt

3/4 cup grated extra-sharp Cheddar cheese

SCALLOPED TOMATOES

INGREDIENTS

5 tablespoons butter

1 green pepper,
cored, seeded,
halved lengthwise,
and cut into half
rings

1 medium Spanish
onion, halved and
sliced into half
rings

1½ cups dry bread
crumbs

6 ripe tomatoes,
washed, cored,
and cut into ¼″–
½″ slices

1½ teaspoons salt

¾ teaspoon pepper

Whenever I came to visit, I always felt a special welcome when Nanny served Scalloped Tomatoes. This clever combination of seasonings for grilled tomatoes was, as far as I was concerned, happy food!

METHOD

Preheat the oven to 325°F. Butter an 8″ to 9″ baking dish.

In a skillet melt 2 tablespoons butter and sauté the green pepper and onion until soft.

Sprinkle the baking dish with about a quarter of the bread crumbs. Cover with a third of the tomato slices. Cover with a third of the pepper and onion. Season with ½ teaspoon salt and ¼ teaspoon pepper. Sprinkle with a quarter of the bread crumbs. Dot with 1 tablespoon butter. Repeat twice, making 3 layers of the vegetables in all. Bake for 45 to 60 minutes, or until tender.

YIELD · 6–8 SERVINGS

FRIED ZUCCHINI

INGREDIENTS

Vegetable oil for
frying

4 zucchini, washed
and cut into ⅛″–¼″
slices

1 cup milk

1 cup all-purpose flour

1 teaspoon salt

1 teaspoon pepper

1 teaspoon paprika

Fried Zucchini cooks up like cottage fries in this straightforward recipe. The addition of paprika turns these crispy fries into spicy treats. For a change, try Fried Zucchini whenever you might serve French fries. They're terrific with fish or chicken. In some parts of the West, fried zucchini is even served with barbecue.

METHOD

In a deep fryer heat the oil to 375°F.

Dip the zucchini in the milk and then lightly in the flour.

Deep-fry in batches until golden brown, 2 to 3 minutes. Reheat the oil to 375° between batches. Drain on paper towels.

In a shaker mix together the salt, pepper, and paprika; sprinkle over the fries. Serve hot.

YIELD · 4–6 SERVINGS

LILLIE'S ZUCCHINI AND SUMMER SQUASH AU GRATIN

Lillie's colorful casserole is a lot like the colorful bouquets she arranges throughout the Headquarters, just as Nanny did years ago. Her knack for color and natural combinations comes through in this medley of tomatoes, summer squash, and zucchini laced with Parmesan. The mild flavors and pastel colors of this barely seasoned dish are really very nice with delicate chicken or fish.

METHOD

Preheat the oven to 325°F. Butter a 3-quart casserole or baking dish.

In a pot with water to cover, boil the squash and zucchini until just tender, 5 to 10 minutes. When cooked, place a layer of squash in the casserole or baking dish. Top with a layer of tomatoes. Sprinkle with some of the salt and pepper. Repeat until all the vegetables and seasonings are used. Sprinkle the top layer with grated cheese. Bake for 40 minutes. Top with the bread crumbs, dot with butter, and run under the broiler to brown.

YIELD · 4–6 SERVINGS

INGREDIENTS

- 1 pound summer squash, cut into ¾" chunks
- 1 pound zucchini, cut into ¾" chunks
- 1 pound tomatoes, peeled and cut into ¾" chunks
- 1 teaspoon salt
- ½ teaspoon pepper
- ½ cup grated Parmesan cheese
- ½ cup dry bread crumbs
- 1 tablespoon butter

SIDE DISHES

GRITS SOUFFLÉ

Grits are a southern staple, but I've never tasted any like the kind that Nanny made by adapting a recipe of unknown origin entitled "Grits Maryland." They're a bit more trouble to make but produce a sweet soufflé that's well worth the extra effort. They're as complementary to ham as candied yams. Served with roast beef, they're an elegant surprise. And for breakfast, these grits are a treat and can be cooked ahead and then reheated as needed.

INGREDIENTS

2 *cups water*
1 *teaspoon salt*
¾ *cup hominy grits*
2 *cups milk*
1 *egg, separated*
4 *tablespoons butter*
1 *tablespoon sugar*

METHOD

Bring the water to a boil over direct heat in the top saucepan of a double boiler, and whisk in the salt and hominy grits. Stirring constantly, bring to a boil and continue to boil for 2 minutes. Stir in 1 cup milk until smooth. Bring to a simmer, then place the pan over the bottom of the double boiler and cook gently for an hour, stirring occasionally.

Preheat the oven to 325°F. Butter a 1-quart baking dish. Beat the egg yolk. Remove the grits from the heat, add the butter, sugar, egg yolk, and remaining milk. Blend well. Just before baking, beat the egg white until stiff but not dry and gently fold into the mixture. Pour into the baking dish and bake for 1 hour.

YIELD · 4–6 SERVINGS

CHEESE GRITS

Most recipes for cheese grits call for garlic and cooking the grits until the cheese melts and the two main ingredients are well blended. Nanny's recipe, though, contains one of her clever shortcuts that produces a sharper, more cheesy result. First, the grits are made "a la Maryland" but without sugar, and then sharp grated cheese is added just before baking. The grits are predictably pleasing with ham, and equally good with ribs or pork barbecue.

INGREDIENTS

1 recipe Grits Soufflé (page 172) without sugar

1 teaspoon salt

1 cup grated Cheddar cheese

½ teaspoon pepper

METHOD

Follow the recipe for Grits Soufflé, cooking the grits in a double boiler for an hour.

Preheat the oven to 325°F. Butter a 1-quart baking dish.

Remove the grits from the heat, and add the remaining ingredients (except the sugar): the additional salt, the cheese, and pepper. Pour into the baking dish and bake for 1 hour.

YIELD · 4–6 SERVINGS

CHEESE SOUFFLÉ

As a party dish, this recipe is light and impressive in appearance. Nanny served it as a buffet item or occasionally as a light supper with salad and dessert. Slow cooking on low heat makes the texture quite soft. Yet the soufflé still makes a spectacular ascent, growing high and full over the side of the soufflé dish to wind up looking much like a French chef's toque. A word to the wise: If you divide this recipe into smaller soufflés, don't fill the soufflé dishes more than three-quarters full!

INGREDIENTS

4 tablespoons butter
4 1/2 tablespoons flour
1 1/2 cups milk
1 teaspoon salt
Dash cayenne
1/2 pound sharp
Cheddar or
Gruyère cheese,
grated
6 eggs, separated

METHOD

Preheat the oven to 300°F. Generously butter a 2-quart souf-flé dish.

In a heavy-bottomed saucepan melt the butter. Add the flour and stir until smooth. Pour in the milk, stirring until smooth. Add the salt and cayenne. Cook and stir until smooth and thick. Take the pan off the heat and add the cheese; stir until melted and smooth. Add the egg yolks and beat until smooth. Let the mixture cool while beating the egg whites stiff. Fold the whites into the yolk mixture and turn into the soufflé dish. Bake for 1 1/4 hours.

YIELD · 4 SERVINGS

SPAGHETTI AND CHEESE

Ranch Fried steak just wouldn't be the same without Nanny's Spaghetti and Cheese. A bit drier than the average macaroni and cheese casserole, the mustard and Worcestershire called for in Nanny's version really wakes up this typically mild dish. Why spaghetti is used rather than elbows, is anybody's guess. It's just one of those quirky traditions that made any other way just wouldn't be the same.

INGREDIENTS

3/4 pound spaghetti
3 ounces sharp
Cheddar cheese, cut
into 1/4" cubes
1 teaspoon dry
mustard
3 cups Cheddar
Cheese Sauce (page
178) made with 3/4
tablespoon
Worcestershire
sauce

METHOD

Preheat the oven to 350°F. Butter a 2-quart casserole.

Cook the spaghetti in a pot of boiling water according to the package directions. Drain well. Place in the casserole. Mix two-thirds of the cheese cubes in with the spaghetti. Pour the cheese sauce evenly over the spaghetti. Top with the remaining cheese cubes and bake for 20 to 30 minutes, or until hot and bubbly.

YIELD · 8 SERVINGS

SAUCES
AND
MARINADES

The Panhandle saw hard times in the 1930s. Drought and pestilence created dust bowls, making farming and ranching all but impossible. Crops were destroyed by too much sun and too little rain. Then, loose topsoil unanchored by ground cover was swept away by incessant winds that caused blinding, choking sand and dust storms called "Black Dusters." Fields were left unarable; parched pastures were covered with dust and sand, leaving cattle nothing to eat. The local economy was shattered.

Some local folk just quipped, "The Depression wouldn't a-been so bad if it hadn't a-come at such hard times," but the fact was, many farmers, and not a few ranchers, went under. However, Martha and Ted Houghton persevered for almost ten years through the hard times that lasted until World War II.

Good times returned with the end of the war. The forties and fifties were happy, productive years at the Ranch and were only interrupted by one nearly catastrophic incident. In 1950, a raging prairie fire almost destroyed the Headquarters. The fire is believed to have been started by sunlight that burned through broken glass onto dry grass. Seventy-five-mile-an-hour winds bellowed the fire and caused it to jump a forty-foot roadway where it quickly spread to the oasis. The great cottonwoods caught fire along with barns and pens that burned to the ground. Had it not been for the Dalhart Fire Department, which sped over forty miles of farm roads to the Ranch, the Headquarters would have been destroyed.

Needless to say, many treasures would have been lost, including most of Nanny's recipes. Among those that would have been missed most is Nanny's rare, old recipe for Barbecue Sauce, a tangy, sweet condiment with a spirit all its own.

Another more recent recipe, Gar's Chili Salsa, could start a fire of its own. It arrived with Lillie and Gar when they came to the Ranch in 1975. As salsas go, it's pure heat and adds a special touch to any Tex-Mex dish. Chili just isn't the same without it.

Even Nanny, who was well into her eighties when Lillie and Gar came to the Ranch, thought Gar's Chili Salsa was sensational. Most elderly people avoid spicy food, but Nanny would dab a little on her meat or enchiladas and enjoy it right along with the rest of us.

Hot or sweet, the recipes here are as versatile as they are unusual. The barbecue sauce and marinade, when used together, work as well for chicken and shrimp as they do for beef and pork. Gar's Salsa is more than a Tex-Mex condiment; it's a catalyst for chili or Son of a Gun Stew. The rest, as usual, are Nanny's favorites that just "go" with her West Texas country cooking.

SAUCES

NANNY'S "J.J." BARBECUE SAUCE

Most barbecue sauces are spicy hot and carry warnings like "mean," "madness," or "inferno." Nanny's favorite recipe for barbecue sauce, though, was spicy sweet. It's so old, the original "method" calls for putting up the sauce "in sterilized bottles sealed with new corks and hot wax"!

METHOD

In a pot simmer the tomatoes for 30 minutes to reduce to a pulp; put through a sieve or the fine disc of a food mill to remove the skins and seeds.

In a pot combine the tomato pulp, onions, and the remaining ingredients and simmer for 1½ hours, until medium thick, and reduced by half, stirring frequently.

Cool and refrigerate, or preserve according to proper canning techniques.

YIELD · 1 ½ QUARTS

INGREDIENTS

4 pounds tomatoes, washed and quartered

3 small onions, minced

½ tablespoon salt

½ tablespoon pepper

½ tablespoon ground ginger

½ tablespoon ground allspice

1 cup brown sugar

1 cup cider vinegar

BRANDY SAUCE FOR PANCAKES

INGREDIENTS

2 *eggs*

1 *cup powdered sugar*

1/2 *teaspoon vanilla extract*

3 *tablespoons butter, room temperature*

2 *tablespoons heavy cream*

1 *tablespoon brandy*

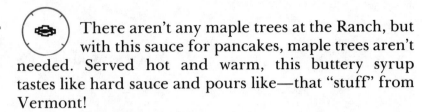 There aren't any maple trees at the Ranch, but with this sauce for pancakes, maple trees aren't needed. Served hot and warm, this buttery syrup tastes like hard sauce and pours like—that "stuff" from Vermont!

M E T H O D

In a bowl beat the eggs until thick. Beat in the powdered sugar until thick. Add the remaining ingredients and mix well. Keep warm over hot water, but don't cook.

YIELD · 1 CUP

CHEDDAR CHEESE SAUCE

INGREDIENTS

2 *tablespoons butter*

2 *tablespoons flour*

2 *cups milk*

1 1/2 *cups shredded Cheddar cheese*

Salt and pepper

Pinch grated nutmeg

1 *teaspoon dry mustard (optional)*

3/4 *tablespoon Worcestershire sauce (optional)*

When Martha Houghton wanted to highlight fresh steamed vegetables such as broccoli or cauliflower or add an elegant touch to a favorite casserole, she often used this simple recipe for a smooth cheese sauce flavored with a good, sharp Cheddar. This sauce is particularly nice on Baked Lima Beans and Ruby Wagner's Deviled Egg Casserole.

M E T H O D

In a saucepan melt the butter over moderate heat. Add the flour and stir until smooth. Pour in the milk, stir until smooth, and cook, stirring, until thickened. Simmer for 5 minutes, remove from the heat, and stir in the cheese until melted. Season to taste with salt, pepper, and a pinch nutmeg. A little mustard and Worcestershire sauce may be added.

YIELD · 3 CUPS

CREAM GRAVY

Chuck-wagon cooks have always been the butt of cowboy humor. Cream Gravy reminds me of the toothless wrangler who carried his dentures in his pocket. They said the only time he used them was to chew the cook's gravy! Properly made, this gravy adds a classic "Texan touch" to Ranch Fried Steak or Fried Chicken. It's also quite nice on dove or quail.

METHOD

Drain off all but 1 tablespoon oil or fat from a roasting or frying pan used to make Ranch Fried Steak, Fried Chicken, or any roasted bird. Stir in the flour until smooth. Add the cream, milk, and chicken broth, and stir until smooth. Heat to the boil, stirring and scraping any bits off the pan bottom, and simmer for 5 minutes, until thickened and smooth. Season to taste with salt and pepper. Serve at once.

YIELD · 1 ¾ CUPS

INGREDIENTS

1   tablespoon oil or fat
2   tablespoons flour
²/₃ cup heavy cream
²/₃ cup milk
½ cup chicken broth
    Salt and pepper

GAME SAUCE FOR PRAIRIE CHICKEN

INGREDIENTS

1 cup chicken broth

1 tablespoon butter

1 1/2 tablespoons flour

1/4 cup light cream

*1 tablespoon dry
sherry or to taste*

1/2 teaspoon salt

1/8 teaspoon pepper

*1/2 teaspoon ground
sage*

*1/2 teaspoon lemon
juice*

 Sage and sherry make this sauce an elegant complement to Prairie Chicken (page 124) or any other upland game, really. Its earthy aroma also reminds me of the wild sage at the Ranch that stretches along the range for miles and makes the pastures look like silver-green plush carpets.

For all its ethereal qualities, this sauce is quite easy to make. Just spike your pan gravy with a little sage, sherry, and lemon to taste.

METHOD

Drain the grease from the roasting pan used for Prairie Chicken. Add the chicken broth to the pan and place over heat, scraping the sides and bottom of the pan to loosen the drippings. Skim off any remaining grease. Set the pan aside while making the roux.

In a saucepan melt the butter and stir in the flour until blended. Pour in the chicken broth and drippings from the roasting pan, and cook, stirring constantly, until the mixture is smooth. Add the cream and cook until the sauce bubbles and thickens. Add the sherry, seasonings, and lemon juice. Stir and serve in a warm gravy boat.

YIELD · ABOUT 1 CUP

SALSAS

GAR'S CHILI SALSA

With Lillie and Gar's arrival, this chili salsa became the favorite hot condiment at the Ranch. Frequently served with any of the Tex-Mex recipes, it is equally complementary to scrambled eggs or roast beef. You may shed a few tears when you make it, then again you may shed a few more when you run out.

M E T H O D

Chop the peppers, onions, and tomatoes in batches in a blender or a food processor, until ¼″ to ⅛″ dice—the consistency should be similar to coarse soup or minced coleslaw. Add batches to a large saucepan as they are chopped. Mix well and add the salt and sugar. Bring to a boil, slowly, stirring occasionally, and simmer for 15 minutes. Refrigerate or seal in jars according to proper canning techniques.

Y I E L D · 1 ¼ Q U A R T S

I N G R E D I E N T S

- 4 cups halved jalapeño peppers (about 30 peppers, 2″–2½″ long)
- 2 medium onions, coarsely chopped
- 2 pounds tomatoes, washed and coarsely chopped
- 1 teaspoon salt
- 2 teaspoons sugar

SALSA RANCHERA

INGREDIENTS

12 *large tomatoes,
cored, peeled, and
chopped*

2 *large onions,
chopped*

4 *green peppers,
seeded and chopped*

2 *tablespoons salt*

4 *tablespoons brown
sugar*

2 *tablespoons ground
ginger*

1 *tablespoon ground
cinnamon*

1 *tablespoon dry
mustard*

1 *tablespoon grated
nutmeg*

1 *quart cider vinegar*

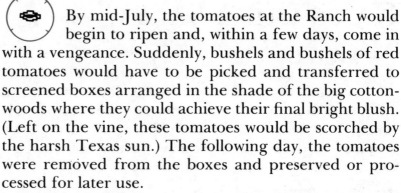 By mid-July, the tomatoes at the Ranch would begin to ripen and, within a few days, come in with a vengeance. Suddenly, bushels and bushels of red tomatoes would have to be picked and transferred to screened boxes arranged in the shade of the big cottonwoods where they could achieve their final bright blush. (Left on the vine, these tomatoes would be scorched by the harsh Texas sun.) The following day, the tomatoes were removed from the boxes and preserved or processed for later use.

Countless bushels of tomatoes—probably a wagon load or two over the years—made their way into this "Ranch-style" sauce. Its flavor hovers somewhere between a sharp catsup and a mild salsa picante but gets its spirit from cinnamon, dry mustard, and vinegar rather than chiles or jalapeños.

As a condiment, this sauce really sets off hamburgers, fresh pork, or Huevos Rancheros.

METHOD

Place all the vegetables in a pot and add the remaining ingredients. Boil for 3 hours, or until thick, stirring frequently. Cool and refrigerate, or preserve according to proper canning techniques.

YIELD · 2½ QUARTS

MARINADES

NANNY'S "J.J." BARBECUE MARINADE

"J.J." comes from the days when the Ranch was known as the J.J. Division of the 248,000-acre spread owned by Martha Houghton's father, John M. Shelton. In those times, pastures were rated for their quality of grazing and the best were called "J.J." as in "just the best for just about anything." We think Nanny's marinade deserves a "J.J." rating of its own.

METHOD

Mix all the ingredients, except the oil, well. Whisk in a little oil at a time to make a creamy marinade. If using a blender, add oil in a thin, continuous stream at low speed.

YIELD · 2 CUPS

INGREDIENTS

1/3 cup cider vinegar

3 tablespoons Worcestershire sauce

1 3/4 teaspoons dry mustard

2 cloves garlic, minced

1 tablespoon brown sugar

1 cup vegetable oil

RED GAME MARINADE

1 cup beer

1 cup dry red
wine

1 bay leaf

8–10 peppercorns

1 onion, sliced

1 teaspoon
crushed dried
rosemary

1 clove garlic,
minced

1 stalk celery with
leaves,
quartered

1 carrot,
quartered

Anything that's wild and runs on four legs can benefit from a "bath" in this solution before cooking. A reliable tenderizer, it's also quite useful in sauces or gravies.

M E T H O D

In a glass or ceramic container mix the ingredients. Marinate steaks or chops for 2 to 3 hours at room temperature, or 4 to 6 hours in the refrigerator if the weather is hot.

NOTE: *For roasts or large chunks of meat, double the quantities and the marinating time.*

YIELD · 2 ½ CUPS · ENOUGH FOR 2 –3 POUNDS GAME SLICED 1″ THICK

MARINADE FOR WATERFOWL

1 cup apple cider

1 ½ cups dry red wine

8 juniper berries,
crushed

¼ teaspoon ground
sage
(continued)

Whether you fry, broil, or even smoke your waterfowl, this marinade will enhance the results. It helps tenderize the flesh, deflect some of the gaminess, and contribute great flavor to your sauces. The juniper berries, sage, and cloves add a woodsy aroma that's just a bit sharp on the palate, while the cider and red wine soften the flesh as well as impart a piquant, fruity taste.

METHOD

In a glass or ceramic container mix the ingredients. Marinate the fowl for 2 days, refrigerated.

YIELD · 3 CUPS · ENOUGH FOR 4 DUCK BREASTS, 2 DUCKS, OR 1 CANADA GOOSE

1 onion, sliced

2 garlic cloves, minced

1 bay leaf

1 celery stalk with leaves, sliced

1 carrot, sliced

1/2 teaspoon salt

1/2 teaspoon pepper

Rosy Mayonnaise

The paprika in Nanny's recipe gives this mayonnaise a rosy tint not unlike sunsets in the fall on the High Plains. That's a good time to make it, because this mayonnaise goes so well with game.

METHOD

By hand: In a bowl beat the egg yolks, salt, pepper, sugar, and mustard together. Add the vinegar and mix well. Add the paprika and mix well. While continuously beating, pour in oil slowly, drop by drop, and continue beating until thoroughly mixed. Refrigerate.

By food processor: Place the eggs, salt, pepper, sugar, and mustard in the workbowl and process for 30 seconds. Add the vinegar and paprika and process for another 30 seconds, until mixed well. With the machine on, slowly pour the oil through the feed tube in one thin, steady stream, until the mixture has emulsified and the mayonnaise is made.

YIELD · 2 CUPS

INGREDIENTS

2 egg yolks or 1 whole egg plus 1 yolk if using food processor

3/4 teaspoon salt

1/4 teaspoon pepper

1/4 teaspoon sugar

1/4 teaspoon dry mustard

1/4 cup wine vinegar

2 tablespoons paprika

1 1/2 cups vegetable oil

3 teasp = 1 tablesp.

6 teasp = 1 ounce

16 tea sp = 1/3 cup –

2 table sp. = 1 ounce

4 table sp = 1/4 cup

5 1/3 table sp = 1/3 cup.

1 cup = 1/2 Pint

cup –1 pt = 1/4 lb –

1 cup = 8 ounces.

DESSERTS

Throughout the sixties and early seventies, my visits to the Ranch always ended by having dinner with Nanny's mother, Mrs. I. C. Thurmond. Like Nanny's desserts, these meals were pleasant finales to my summer vacations.

"Grandmother," as she liked to be called, was 103 when she passed on in December 1976. Lucid and well-informed through her final years, her bearing was regal and genteel. Her silver-white hair was always perfectly coiffed, her aged complexion almost lily white. Seated at the head of her table, she'd hold forth in her soft, gravelly southern drawl and regale us with stories about the earliest days of cattle ranching in the Panhandle.

Sour Cream Cake

2 eggs, 1 scant cup sugar 1 cup flour
1/4 teaspoon soda 1 level teaspoon B.
powder pin & salt vanilla
Break eggs into cup and fill
up with sour cream Beat well,
add sugar and beat again, and go
on and make your cake.

Grandmother's recollections were spellbinding: the wild and woolly days of Amarillo's precursor, Old Tascosa, where Billy the Kid spent a few final days of his own; or the appearance of the telephone and the refusal of many to believe that such a device had been invented. When Grandmother talked about the early, dusty days of Amarillo, and how thousands of cattle jammed into railhead pens of the Santa Fe bawled incessantly through sweltering nights, you were there.

Grandmother was just as partial to desserts as she was to history. She was especially fond of meringue and her recipes for Meringue Torte, Meringue Kisses, and Meringue Topping for pies were included in Nanny's extensive collection.

In Grandmother's day—and Nanny's—desserts were more than a delicious finish, they also provided a quick lift from big, heavy meals before returning to hard work in the fields or on horseback.

Today, ranch life is not as strenuous as it used to be, but no one has lost his appetite for these sweet treats. Some are quite inventive, such as Alva T.'s lemon-flavored 7-Up Cake or Sweet Potato Pudding with raisins. Others are old-fashioned favorites, such as Peach Cobbler and Aunt Phemia's Sugar Cookies. For today's pace, though, more than a few are quick-to-fix, such as Frozen Mocha Cheesecake and Apricot Tapioca Cream.

OPPOSITE AND PAGE 186: MEASUREMENT CONVERSIONS AND A RECIPE FROM NANNY'S COLLECTION IN HER OWN HAND— WRITTEN DOWN ANYWHERE CONVENIENT

CAKES AND ICINGS

ALVA T.'S 7-UP CAKE

This is it. Created by Alva T. Franklin, Nanny's Amarillo cook for almost 40 years, 7-Up Cake is practically a staple at the Houghton Ranch. Alva T. still lovingly bakes and sends them out to the Ranch where the cake briefly occupies an exalted place on the kitchen counter. There, a knife is left on the cake plate for all those who "happen" to pass by and can't live until the next meal. All the tracks left between the kitchen door and counter, though, show that most just "happen" by for a piece of Alva T.'s cake.

INGREDIENTS

1½ cups (3 sticks) butter or margarine, room temperature

3 cups sugar

5 eggs, room temperature

3 cups cake flour

2 tablespoons pure lemon extract

¾ cup 7-Up, room temperature

METHOD

Preheat the oven to 350°F. Place the rack in the lower third of the oven. Grease and flour a 10″ tube pan.

Cream the butter in a bowl with an electric mixer at medium speed for 30 seconds. With the mixer running at medium speed, slowly add the sugar and continue creaming for 3 to 4 minutes longer. Again at medium speed, add the eggs, one at a time, creaming after each addition. Continue creaming for another 2 minutes.

Using a rubber spatula, fold the flour in gradually, about a third at a time, mixing gently but thoroughly. Fold in the lemon extract and 7-Up a third at a time.

Pour the mixture into the prepared pan, smooth the top, and bake for 1¼ hours, or until a toothpick inserted in the middle comes out clean and the cake begins to withdraw from the sides of the pan.

Cool on a wire rack for 15 minutes. Remove from the pan and cool thoroughly on a wire rack. Slice with a serrated knife.

YIELD · 16–20 SERVINGS

ALMOND-COCONUT
SNOW CAKE

Laced with sherry or amaretto, this frozen pudding "cake" is not unlike bisquet tortoni. It's very light, elegantly trimmed with ladyfingers, and quite clean on the palate.

METHOD

Line a 2-quart soufflé dish with plastic wrap, leaving the ends hanging out over the sides of the dish. Place the ladyfingers all around the dish, crust sides out. Place any extra ladyfingers, crust side down, evenly over the bottom. Just before filling the lined dish, pour 1 tablespoon sherry into a ramekin, and using a pastry brush, lightly paint the ladyfingers with the sherry.

In a bowl beat the egg yolks until light. Add the sugar and remaining 2 tablespoons sherry and mix well. Add the crumbled macaroons and mix well. Beat the egg whites until stiff, and whip the cream until stiff. Fold the egg whites and cream into the yolk mixture and pour into the prepared dish. Place more plastic wrap over the top and freeze for at least 6 hours.

Unmold by using the ends of the plastic wrap to free the cake. Serve immediately.

YIELD · 8 SERVINGS

INGREDIENTS

- *1 package ladyfingers, unseparated*
- *3 tablespoons sherry*
- *3 eggs, separated*
- *½ cup powdered sugar*
- *6 almond macaroons, crumbled*
- *2 cups whipping cream*

CHOCOLATE LOG

In France, a similar but more elaborate choco-late roll cake is known as bûche de Noël, and served on Christmas. At the Ranch, it's a Chocolate Log that's featured more than once a year. Long and brown, its parched surface looks like bark on a tree, but the cake itself has a nice cocoa taste and the texture is nice and "spongy." As a buffet dessert, the log makes a stunning centerpiece.

- 4 eggs, separated
- ¾ cup granulated sugar
- 4 tablespoons cake flour
- 6 tablespoons unsweetened cocoa powder
- ½ teaspoon baking powder
- 2–4 tablespoons powdered sugar
- 1 cup whipping cream

METHOD

Preheat the oven to 400°F. Grease a 10"-×-15" shallow baking pan, line with waxed paper, and then grease the paper.

In a bowl beat the egg yolks with the granulated sugar until thick and lemon colored. In a separate bowl sift together the flour, cocoa, and baking powder.

Whip the egg whites until stiff. Fold half the whites into the yolks. Fold in half the cocoa mixture. Repeat with the whites and cocoa. Spread the batter evenly in prepared pan. Bake for 12 minutes.

Remove the pan from the oven and cool on a wire rack for 5 minutes. Spread out a clean dish towel and sprinkle with 1 tablespoon powdered sugar. Invert the cake pan on the towel, removing the cake from the pan, and carefully peel off the waxed paper. Cool briefly to room temperature (see Note).

Meanwhile, make the filling. Whip the cream until it holds a shape, sweeten to taste with the powdered sugar, and spread over the cooled cake. Roll up and refrigerate until serving time.

NOTE: If you do not wish to fill the cake right away, roll it in a towel, starting with the long side, and let it cool, rolled. When ready to fill, unroll carefully, spread the filling, and reroll.

YIELD · 8 SERVINGS

DEVIL'S FOOD CAKE

Leaving out this recipe for Devil's Food Cake would be like forgetting to serve dessert at the Houghton Ranch—unforgivable!

As devil's food goes, Nanny's version is light and fluffy. With the yolks and beaten whites folded in separately, it rises higher than most. Dressed with her Chocolate Mousse Frosting, it's two desserts in one.

M E T H O D

Preheat the oven to 350°F. Butter and flour two 9" round cake pans.

In a bowl cream the butter for 1 minute. Gradually add the sugar and cream for 2 minutes. Add the egg yolks and beat for 1 minute. Add the melted chocolate and beat for 1 minute more. Stir in the sour cream and beat until well combined.

In another bowl sift the flour and baking soda together. Sift a third of the flour onto the chocolate mixture and fold in. Add half the milk and mix in. Sift on another third of the flour and fold in. Add the vanilla. Stir in the other half of the milk, then the last third of the flour. Beat the egg whites until stiff and fold into the batter.

Divide the batter evenly between the 2 prepared pans and bake for 35 to 45 minutes, or until a cake tester inserted in the middle comes out clean.

Cool in pans on a wire rack for 10 minutes. Remove from the pans and cool thoroughly. Meanwhile, make the frosting. Frost and serve.

YIELD · ONE 9" LAYER CAKE
12–16 SERVINGS

INGREDIENTS

- *1 cup butter, room temperature*
- *2 cups granulated sugar*
- *5 eggs, separated*
- *5 ounces unsweetened chocolate, melted*
- *1 cup sour cream*
- *2 cups cake flour*
- *1 teaspoon baking soda*
- *¾ cup milk*
- *2 teaspoons vanilla extract*
- *1 recipe Chocolate Mousse Frosting (page 200)*

FROZEN MOCHA CHEESE CAKE

INGREDIENTS

- *1¼ cups chocolate cookie crumbs (5 ounces cookies)*
- *¼ cup granulated sugar*
- *¼ cup butter or margarine, melted and cooled to room temperature*
- *1 8-ounce package cream cheese*
- *⅔ cup chocolate syrup*
- *1 14-ounce can condensed milk*
- *2 tablespoons instant coffee dissolved in 1 teaspoon hot water*
- *1 cup whipping cream*

Martha Houghton's collection of recipes for chocolate confections was extensive, but this is my favorite. It's quite easy to make, and the result is elegant. With the exception of melting butter for the crust, this recipe requires no cooking. What you get is a velvety icebox cake deftly flavored with chocolate and coffee and pleasantly cheesy.

METHOD

In a bowl combine the cookie crumbs, sugar, and butter and place on the bottom of a 9″ springform pan. Pat into a crust.

In a food processor or large bowl beat the cream cheese until fluffy. Add the chocolate syrup and condensed milk. Mix in the dissolved coffee. Whip the cream and fold into the chocolate mixture. Pour into the pan and freeze for 6 hours or until firm. Serve frozen.

YIELD · 8–12 SERVINGS

FUDGE CAKE

Just a little more "cakelike" than brownies, this recipe calls for unsweetened chocolate and makes a cake that's pleasantly dark and not cloyingly sweet.

METHOD

Preheat the oven to 350°F. Butter an 8″ square pan.

Cream the butter for 1 minute. Add the sugar gradually and cream for 2 minutes more. Add the eggs and cream for another minute.

Sift the flour and salt over the butter mixture and fold in. Add the melted chocolate and fold in. Add the vanilla and nuts and fold in.

Pour the batter into the pan and bake for 30 minutes. Cool in the pan and cut into 2″ squares.

YIELD · 16 SQUARES

INGREDIENTS

- ½ cup butter
- 1 cup granulated sugar
- 2 eggs
- 1 cup cake flour
- ⅛ teaspoon salt
- 2 ounces unsweetened chocolate, melted
- 1 teaspoon vanilla extract
- 1½ cups coarsely chopped walnuts

GEE, IT WAS FUN TO BE A KID AT THE RANCH!

GRANDMOTHER'S MERINGUE TORTE

INGREDIENTS

8 egg whites

1 1/2 cups granulated sugar

1 teaspoon white vinegar

1 teaspoon vanilla extract

OPTIONAL:

Fresh or preserved fruits

Whipped cream

NANNY'S MOTHER, MRS. I. C. THURMOND, ABOUT 1915. TO GRANDCHILDREN, GREAT-GRANDCHILDREN, AND THEIR MANY FRIENDS, SHE LIKED TO BE CALLED "GRANDMOTHER."

Sometimes Grandmother's great luncheons included her Meringue Torte for dessert, with ice cream and a thick fruit sauce made by combining ripe fruit and rich preserves. It was as lively as our discussions of current events and intriguing as Grandmother's recollections of the early Amarillo days.

METHOD

Preheat the oven to 300°F. Grease the bottoms only of two 9" to 10" springform pans and place a circle of brown paper on each bottom. Cake pans with removable bottoms may be used instead. If cake pans are used, grease, then place a circle of brown paper on the bottom. Make 2" collars of brown paper and line the sides with the collars.

In a bowl beat the egg whites until stiff. Add the sugar very gradually, about 2 tablespoons at a time. Add the vinegar and vanilla and beat well. Spread the meringue evenly in the

prepared pans. Bake for 15 minutes, then lower heat to 225° and bake for 45 minutes. Let cool in the oven.

Serve with fresh or preserved fruits and whipped cream, if desired.

NOTE: *The vinegar keeps the center of the meringue soft and fluffy. To use as a crunchy tart shell, place the mixture on a cookie sheet or shallow baking pan and shape it into a circle. For a higher, "gooier" meringue (to serve with ice cream), place the mixture in a springform pan.*

YIELD · 12—16 SERVINGS

SOUR CREAM CAKE

True to form this simple classic cake turned up on the back of an envelope. It makes a wonderfully moist, spongy white cake that's as pleasing as coffee cake when served warm, or just right with a cold glass of milk when cooled and topped with Nanny's crunchy, sweet Chocolate Pecan Icing.

METHOD

Preheat the oven to 350°F. Grease a 9″ cake pan.

Beat eggs and sour cream together until well mixed. Add the sugar and beat for 1 minute. Add vanilla and mix well.

Sift the flour, baking soda, baking powder, and salt into the egg mixture. Stir in thoroughly.

Pour batter into prepared pan and bake for 25 to 30 minutes, or until a cake tester (knife) comes out clean.

Remove from pan and serve warm as a coffee cake, or cool on a wire rack and frost when cool. Nanny's Chocolate Pecan Icing (page 202) is a good choice. For coffee cake, sprinkle with sugar and cinnamon to taste just before baking.

YIELD · 8 SERVINGS

INGREDIENTS

2 eggs
½ cup sour cream
1 cup sugar
1 teaspoon vanilla
1 cup flour
¼ teaspoon baking soda
1 teaspoon baking powder
Pinch salt

JOSIE CAKE

¾ cup butter

1½ cups granulated
sugar

4 eggs

3 cups cake flour

2½ teaspoons baking
powder

1⅓ cups milk

1 recipe Chocolate
Mousse Frosting
(page 200)

If there is one thing central to country cooking, it's the capacity for turning out so many
different recipes using a relatively small number of staples or widely available ingredients. Martha Houghton's
Josie Cake recipe is a fine example. White cake that
contains no vanilla and no flavoring—just butter, sugar,
milk, flour, and eggs—becomes a fluffy stage to present
her wonderful Chocolate Mousse Frosting. The cake is
snow white and exceptionally light, and the mousse
frosting meets the needs of the average "chocoholic."

METHOD

Preheat the oven to 350°F. Butter and flour two 9″ cake pans
or a 9″-×-13″ loaf pan.

In a bowl cream the butter for 30 seconds. Add the sugar
and continue creaming for 2 minutes. Add the eggs, one at
a time, beating well after each addition. Beat for 1 minute
more. In another bowl sift the flour and baking powder together. With a rubber spatula, fold about a third of the flour
into the butter mixture. Stir in half the milk. Fold in another
third of the flour. Stir in the remaining milk. Fold in the
remaining flour.

Place the batter in the prepared pans. Bake for 30 to 35
minutes for the layers, 35 to 40 minutes for the loaf pan.
The cake is done when a cake tester comes out clean and the
cake just begins to shrink from the sides of the pan. Cool in
the pans for 15 minutes, turn out, and cool thoroughly.

Make the frosting and frost before serving.

YIELD · 12–16 SERVINGS

WHITE FRUITCAKE

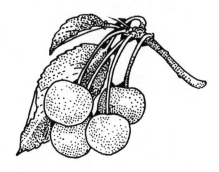

In its original form, this recipe produces 20 pounds of solidly fruited cake. Revised, the ingredients call for twice as much fruit (6¾ pounds) as batter—just enough batter to hold the fruit together. An interesting combination of ingredients, the cake includes almonds and pecans but omits any brandy or rum. The result is moist and light, but requires refrigeration. Don't worry that it won't keep, though. This is one fruitcake that will be eaten long before it needs to depend on spirits to keep it fresh.

METHOD

Preheat the oven to 275°F. Grease a 10″ tube pan and two 9″-×-5″ loaf pans (or 2 tube pans, or 4 loaf pans), line with heavy brown paper, and grease the paper.

In a bowl mix the nuts, fruit, raisins, and coconut with ½ cup flour.

In another bowl cream the butter for 1 minute. Gradually add the sugar and continue creaming for 2 minutes. Add the eggs, one at a time, beating well after each addition, and continue to beat for 2 minutes more. Fold in a third of the remaining flour, then half of the milk, another third of the flour, the rest of the milk, the rest of the flour. Pour the batter over the floured fruits and mix gently but thoroughly.

Spoon the batter into the prepared pans evenly, smooth the tops, and bake in the loaf pans for 2¼ to 2½ hours; in the tube pan for 3 to 3¼ hours. The cakes are done when a cake tester inserted in the middle comes out clean.

Cool the cakes in the pans on a wire rack, then remove from the pans, remove the paper, and wrap airtight to store. Store in the refrigerator.

INGREDIENTS

½ pound shelled almonds

1 pound shelled pecans

1½ pounds candied cherries

1½ pounds candied pineapple, cut in ½″ pieces

¼ pound citron, cut into ¼″ dice

1½ cups golden raisins

½ pound shredded coconut

4 cups cake flour

1 pound butter

2 cups granulated sugar

8 eggs

1 cup milk

YIELD · 30 SERVINGS · ONE RECIPE PRODUCES ENOUGH BATTER TO FILL TWO 2¼-POUND LOAF FRUIT CAKES AND ONE 5¾-POUND TUBE CAKE.

CHOCOLATE MOUSSE/ CHOCOLATE MOUSSE FROSTING

- 1 cup milk
- 1 1/2 cups granulated sugar
- 3 ounces bitter or unsweetened chocolate
- 1 teaspoon unflavored gelatin softened in 2 tablespoons cold water
- 1 1/2 cups heavy cream
- 2 teaspoons vanilla extract

This chocolate confection is light and delicate enough to be enjoyed as mousse and substantial enough to frost any cake regally. If you can't make up your mind, don't worry; the recipe makes enough to frost a two-layer cake plus some extra.

METHOD

In a saucepan combine the milk, sugar, and chocolate; bring to a boil, stirring, and boil for 1 minute. Stir the softened gelatin into the hot chocolate mixture; stir until dissolved. Let cool to room temperature.

Whip the cream until stiff. Add the vanilla to the chocolate mixture and fold in the whipped cream until well blended. Spread on the cooled cake. Or serve chilled as is.

NOTE: *Refrigerate the cake if holding any length of time to maintain the quality of the frosting.*

YIELD · 5 CUPS MOUSSE · OR ENOUGH MOUSSE FROSTING FOR TWO 9" LAYERS

MOCHA ICING

Any number of plain or chocolate cakes will be complemented by Nanny's no-cook, coffee-flavored frosting.

M E T H O D

In a bowl mix the cocoa, butter, and vanilla together. Add about a third of the sugar and moisten with about a quarter of the coffee. Continue adding the sugar and coffee alternately, keeping the mixture a good consistency to spread without running. Be careful not to overmoisten. Beat well. Spread on the cooled cake.

NOTE: *This is very easy to prepare in a food processor.*

YIELD · ABOUT 2 CUPS · ENOUGH FOR TWO 9" LAYERS

INGREDIENTS

2 *rounded tablespoons unsweetened cocoa powder*

2 *tablespoons butter, room temperature*

1 *teaspoon vanilla extract*

3½ *cups powdered sugar*

3–4 *tablespoons strong cold coffee*

CHOCOLATE PECAN ICING

This crunchy-sweet topping is just right for a coarse-grained, spongy cake like Nanny's Sour Cream Cake. A piece with a cold glass of milk is "died and gone to heaven food"—or in this case, "died and gone to the Ranch!"

INGREDIENTS

- 4 tablespoons cocoa powder
- 6 tablespoons milk
- 1 stick margarine or butter, cut into 8 pieces
- 1 pound confectioners' sugar, sifted
- 1 teaspoon vanilla
- 1 cup chopped pecans

METHOD

Place the cocoa in a saucepan. Add the milk gradually, stirring until smooth. Add the margarine and bring the mixture to a boil over medium heat, being careful not to scorch it. Add the sugar and vanilla while mixture is still on the stove and beat well. Stir in the pecans and beat well. Remove pan from heat. Beat a little more and spread hot frosting on the cake.

YIELD · 2 ½ CUPS

CANDY AND COOKIES

"FAT FARM" PEANUT BRITTLE

Before the days of "fat farms" like Neiman-Marcus's Greenhouse and Elizabeth Arden's Maine Chance, well-heeled and well-padded ladies went to sanitoriums or convalescent homes to reduce. In the twenties, Nanny suffered from acute hay fever triggered by the annual fall of cotton seeds that are shed by the giant cottonwoods at the Ranch each spring. To compensate for her discomfort, she turned to Maillard's fancy chocolates, not knowing that the histamines in chocolate only exacerbated her condition. Needless to say, she put on unwanted pounds and eventually checked herself into the Battle Creek Sanitorium up in Michigan. There's no evidence that she received any dietary instruction. However, it's possible to speculate that a major feature of her diet at the sanitorium was fasting. Several of Nanny's sweetest, most fattening recipes were written down on sanitorium stationery—which might lead one to wonder if the ladies swapped recipes as they wiled away the hours without food!

This recipe for peanut brittle was written out on Battle Creek stationery, and is remarkably good. The soda is stirred in at the last minute so the brittle becomes foamy and porous and produces an airy, crunchy candy.

INGREDIENTS

- 2 cups granulated sugar
- 1 cup white Karo syrup
- 2 cups boiling water
- 2 tablespoons butter
- 2 cups shelled peanuts
- 1 teaspoon vanilla extract
- 2 teaspoons baking soda

METHOD

Grease two or three 9″ cake pans.

Boil the sugar, syrup, and water together until it reaches the hard-crack stage, about 295°F on a candy thermometer. Remove from the heat and add the butter and peanuts, and stir for a few minutes. Add the vanilla and soda and beat hard for 1 minute. Pour onto the cake pans and let cool. When cool, break into pieces and store in airtight containers.

YIELD · 2 POUNDS

NANNY'S
TEXAS
TABLE

204

PECAN-DATE ROLLS

Nanny's recipes often pack a wallop. This recipe is a sweet example of how that doesn't always have to mean hot and spicy. One bite of this Pecan-Date Roll and you'll immediately snap to attention. The *Joy of Cooking* recipe for Pecan-Date Rolls calls for adding the dates and nuts last. This recipe cooks the dates down and imparts a strong, sweet flavor. Little thin slices on ice cream make a super topping.

INGREDIENTS

- *3 cups granulated sugar*
- *1 cup milk*
- *10 ounces pitted dates*
- *1 cup chopped pecans*

METHOD

In a large saucepan bring the sugar and milk to a boil and boil for 5 minutes. Stir in the dates and cook for about 30 minutes, until the mixture reaches the soft-ball stage, 238°F on a candy thermometer, or until after beating a spoonful in a small bowl, the mixture will not stick to a wet cloth.

Stir in the pecans and beat until the mixture is creamy. Let cool for a few minutes, then place on aluminum foil and form into 2 rolls. Cool thoroughly and slice to serve.

YIELD · TWO 1-POUND ROLLS

AUNT PHEMIA'S SUGAR COOKIES

Bless Aunt Phemia, whoever she was! No one seems to recall this dear, departed lady, but everyone remembers the great big sugar cookies Nanny made from this mystery woman's recipe. As sugar cookies go, they're crisp, light, and have an almost creamy taste of nutmeg and vanilla. They're also especially simple to make. The recipe produces a soft dough that spreads out into thin "wheels," which bake quite quickly.

In a bowl cream the butter and sugar together until very light. Add the egg and mix until well beaten. Add the vanilla and nutmeg, mixing well. Add the flour and mix well. Chill thoroughly.

Preheat the oven to 400°F. Grease several cookie sheets.

Roll the dough out very thin (⅛″ thickness) using a floured board and floured rolling pin. Cut with a 3″ biscuit cutter and bake on the cookie sheets for 6 to 7 minutes, until light brown. Remove from the sheets and cool on a rack.

YIELD · 72 COOKIES

INGREDIENTS

- *1 cup butter*
- *2 cups granulated sugar*
- *1 egg*
- *1 teaspoon vanilla extract*
- *½ teaspoon grated nutmeg*
- *2 cups all-purpose flour*

MERINGUE KISSES

If Martha Houghton favored chocolate recipes, her mother, Mrs. I. C. Thurmond, was equally devoted to meringue. This recipe for Meringue Kisses includes nuts, coconut, and, of all things, cornflakes! It produces an airy, chewy cookie that has become a real family favorite.

INGREDIENTS

- *4 egg whites*
- *1 cup granulated sugar*
- *1 cup shredded coconut*
- *1 cup chopped nuts*
- *1 teaspoon vanilla extract*
- *3 cups cornflakes*

METHOD

Preheat the oven to 300°F. Grease several cookie sheets.

In a bowl beat the egg whites until stiff. Gradually add the sugar and beat well. Fold in the remaining ingredients and mix well.

Place heaping tablespoonfuls on the cookie sheets and bake until firm and lightly browned, about 30 minutes. Remove from the sheets and cool on a wire rack. Store in an airtight container.

YIELD · 30–36 KISSES

ICEBOX COOKIES

The cookie jar at the Ranch is in the shape of a fat white cat with tan markings. It's always loaded with fresh baked cookies, but a real favorite are these crunchy rounds generously laced with cinnamon and nutmeg. If refrigerated, the dough keeps well for a week and can be baked as needed. Martha Houghton liked that convenience, especially when unexpected company arrived. Served with coffee or tea following afternoon or evening get-togethers, these cookies always got good reviews.

INGREDIENTS

- *1 cup butter (2 sticks)*
- *1 cup brown sugar*
- *1 cup white granulated sugar*
- *2 eggs*
- *3½ cups all-purpose flour*
- *1 teaspoon baking soda*
- *1 teaspoon ground cinnamon*
- *1 teaspoon ground nutmeg*
- *1½ cups chopped nuts (preferably walnuts)*

METHOD

In a bowl cream the butter and sugars together until smooth. Add the eggs and beat until smooth. Sift the flour, soda, cinnamon, and nutmeg together and stir in until smooth. Stir in the nuts.

Form the dough into two rolls, 1½″ to 2″ in diameter, wrap in aluminum foil, and chill for at least 3 hours or overnight.

Preheat the oven to 350°F.

Cut the dough into slices ¼″ thick, and place on an ungreased baking sheet. Bake for 13 to 15 minutes until browned. Remove from the sheet and cool on a wire rack.

YIELD · ABOUT 72 COOKIES

NANNY'S SUGAR COOKIES

Nanny was so fond of sugar cookies that there were various recipes for them throughout her extensive collection. They could be found handwritten on the end papers of her favorite cookbooks or on anything else handy. This version, probably Nanny's favorite, produces thinner and smaller cookies than Aunt Phemia's (see recipe above). The dough is very soft to work with, so thoroughly dust the rolling pin. Crisp and sweet, these are just great with ice cream.

METHOD

In a bowl cream the butter and add the sugar. Cream together until fluffy. Add the eggs, vanilla, and cream and mix well. Sift the flour with the baking powder twice and add to the batter, mixing well. Chill thoroughly.

Preheat the oven to 375°F. Grease several cookies sheets.

On a well-floured board roll out small amounts of the dough to ⅛" thickness, keeping the rest of the dough chilled. Use a well-floured rolling pin. Cut the cookies with a 2½" cutter and place on the prepared sheets. Sprinkle with sugar and bake for 10 to 12 minutes, until browned and crisp.

YIELD · 60–72 COOKIES

INGREDIENTS

- 1 cup butter
- 2 cups granulated sugar
- 2 eggs
- 2 teaspoons vanilla extract
- 2 tablespoons heavy cream
- 2 cups all-purpose flour
- 2 teaspoons baking powder

ICE CREAM AND SHERBET

CHOCOLATE ICE CREAM

In the days before air conditioning in cars, ice cream had to be made at the Ranch. Even with ice chests, anything frozen would melt in 100° heat and the 1½ hours it took to get home from Dalhart. With all the fresh cream, milk, and eggs at the Ranch, though, it seemed a shame to Nanny to buy ice cream anyway. So, long after it was necessary, she continued to make some each week. This recipe produces a version that is distinctly cocoa-like in flavor and pleasantly clean on the palate.

INGREDIENTS

6 *tablespoons sugar*

1 *tablespoon cornstarch*

2 *cups milk*

½ *teaspoon unflavored gelatin softened in 1 tablespoon cold water*

Dash salt

2 *ounces unsweetened chocolate, melted*

1 *tablespoon vanilla extract*

1 *cup heavy cream*

METHOD

In a saucepan mix the sugar and cornstarch. Add the milk gradually, stirring until smooth. Bring to a boil over medium heat, stirring, until thickened. Remove from heat.

Stir the softened gelatin into the hot milk mixture. Add the salt and stir until dissolved. Add the melted chocolate and blend well. Chill.

When cold, stir in the vanilla. Whip the cream just until it forms soft peaks and fold into the chocolate mixture. Freeze until firm in an ice cream maker, according to the manufacturer's directions. The mixture can also be frozen in a metal bowl for 4–6 hours. Stir it every 30 minutes to prevent ice crystals from forming.

YIELD · 1 QUART

MEXICAN ICE CREAM

The colors and textures of this ice cream are festive and fun. The pecans and caramelized sugar contrast well with the ice cream, maraschino cherries and syrup, and in spite of the sweet, sugary ingredients, the taste is surprisingly clean.

Don't expect to make this dessert as quickly as some of Nanny's other ice creams or sherbet. This recipe is not as streamlined as the others and it contains a couple of extra steps. The result is worth it, though. Then again, there may have been more time for more steps when she wrote down her instructions in November 1927.

METHOD

In a heavy bottomed saucepan blend the sugar and cornstarch. Add the eggs and beat to blend well. Stir in the milk until smooth. Cook over medium heat, stirring, until thick and smooth. Remove from heat, cool a little, add the cream and vanilla and cool thoroughly.

Freeze in an ice cream maker according to the manufacturer's directions. When partially frozen, fold in the cherries, syrup, caramelized sugar bits, and pecans, and freeze.

NOTE: *In a heavy saucepan heat ¹/₂ cup sugar with 2 tablespoons water until the sugar melts and turns caramel in color. Pour at once onto a greased cookie sheet and let cool for 10 minutes. Pry off and break into small pieces.*

YIELD · 1 QUART

INGREDIENTS

¹/₄ cup granulated sugar

2 teaspoons cornstarch

2 eggs

2 cups milk

1 cup heavy cream

¹/₂ teaspoon vanilla extract

¹/₂ cup halved maraschino cherries

2 tablespoons maraschino syrup

¹/₂ cup caramelized sugar (see Note)

²/₃ cup chopped pecans

PEACH ICE CREAM

1 quart milk

5 egg yolks

*1 cup granulated
sugar*

*1 teaspoon vanilla
extract*

*2 cups whipped heavy
cream*

*2 cups thinly sliced
peaches*

Served with toasted slices of Alva T.'s 7-Up Cake, this was unforgettable. The peaches were cut in thin slices and added after the ice cream was "cranked," leaving a delicious contrast between the sweet, ripe peaches and soft vanilla ice cream.

METHOD

In a saucepan scald the milk. In a bowl beat the egg yolks with the sugar. Add the milk slowly to the yolks, stirring constantly. Cook in a heavy-bottomed pan or double boiler, stirring, until the custard thickens. Do not boil. Let cool and add the vanilla.

Pour into an ice cream maker and freeze according to the manufacturer's instructions. When the custard starts to freeze, fold in the whipped cream and sliced peaches. Serve semifrozen or slightly soft.

NOTE: *If the peaches are not ripe when purchased, allow to sit in closed brown paper bags at room temperature until the flesh yields to gentle pressure. The added taste and aroma are worth the wait.*

YIELD · 2 QUARTS

MINTED ICE

*1 cup packed fresh
mint leaves,
washed and dried*

1/4 cup lemon juice

*2 cups water
(continued)*

For elaborate dinners, Martha Houghton would sometimes serve minted ice to cleanse the palate between fish and meat courses. The green color is derived from the crème de menthe heightened by food coloring and the taste is far more sophisticated than its preparation—typical Nanny: elegant results achieved through simple cooking.

METHOD

Pound the mint leaves to a pulp or chop finely in a food processor. Add the lemon juice and let the mixture stand for 30 minutes.

In a saucepan boil the water and sugar together for 5 minutes. Pour the sugar syrup over the mint and let stand for 15 minutes. Strain, add the food coloring and the crème de menthe, and freeze in an ice cream machine, according to the manufacturer's directions, or in a metal bowl for 4–6 hours before serving. Stir every 30 minutes if a finer, less slushy, consistency is desired.

YIELD · 1 PINT

1 cup granulated sugar

2–3 drops green food coloring

2 tablespoons crème de menthe

PINEAPPLE SHERBET

Hot summer days and important company always stirred Martha Houghton to serve her famous Pineapple Sherbet. Served in azure-blue hand-blown Mexican dishes, the sherbet was a cool, soothing contrast to her hot, spicy food and the heat outside that could easily top 104° in the shade!

INGREDIENTS

Juice of 3 lemons

3 cups granulated sugar

4 cups milk

1 8¼-ounce can crushed pineapple

METHOD

In a saucepan mix the lemon juice and sugar together and heat until the sugar dissolves. Add the milk and pineapple, undrained.

Chill for an hour, then place in an ice cream maker and freeze according to the manufacturer's directions. Or freeze in a nonbreakable container, stirring every 30 minutes or so, until frozen.

YIELD · 2 QUARTS

PIES

FLAKY PIECRUST

One of the things that makes Nanny's Lemon Meringue Pie so special is its crust. Unlike her Firmer Piecrust, this one is lighter and ideal for pies that do not require as much baking. It's quite nice for Sweet Potato or pudding-type pies.

INGREDIENTS

3½ cups all-purpose flour

½ teaspoon salt

1¼ cups solid vegetable shortening

1 egg, beaten

6 tablespoons cold water

1 tablespoon white vinegar

METHOD

Preheat oven to 425°F.

In a bowl mix the flour and salt together. Cut in the vegetable shortening until the mixture resembles coarse meal. Blend in the egg, water, and vinegar until the mixture forms a dough.

Either chill for an hour before rolling out, or roll out, line pie pans, and chill the crusts for an hour before baking. For recipes that call for prebaked shells, bake 12–15 minutes. Cool before filling.

NOTE: *For baking unfilled crusts,* The Joy of Cooking *recommends "pricking the dough generously with a fork after you have placed it in the pie pan to keep it from leavening and baking unevenly."*

YIELD · TWO 8"–9" PIECRUSTS

FIRMER PIECRUST

Experienced bakers would call the crust produced by this simple recipe "nice and short." The amount of shortening is relatively large and the absence of sugar makes this crust especially solid and even crumbly. If you find it too crumbly to work with, just add a little water as needed. This shell is terrific for mince pie made with Nanny's green tomato mincemeat or any dense fruit pie.

INGREDIENTS

2 cups all-purpose flour

½ teaspoon salt

½ teaspoon baking powder

⅓ cup solid vegetable shortening, cold

⅓ cup unsalted butter, cold

3–4 tablespoons ice water

METHOD

In a bowl or a food processor, mix the flour, salt, and baking powder together. Cut in the shortening and butter until the mixture resembles coarse meal. Add 3 tablespoons ice water and mix until the dough clumps together. If necessary, add the remaining water gradually to get the dough to clump together.

Roll out to ⅛" thickness and fit into 2 pie plates. Chill for an hour to relax the dough before baking or filling.

YIELD · TWO 9" PIECRUSTS

BLACK BOTTOM PIE

CRUST

4 ounces
gingersnaps,
crushed into fine
crumbs

4 tablespoons butter,
melted

CUSTARD

2 cups milk

4 eggs, separated

1 cup granulated
sugar

1¼ tablespoons
cornstarch

1½ ounces
unsweetened
chocolate, melted

1 teaspoon vanilla
extract

1 envelope of
unflavored gelatin
softened in ¼ cup
cold water

½ teaspoon cream of
tartar

1 teaspoon rum
extract or
flavoring, or 2
tablespoons rum
(see Note)

TOPPING

1 cup whipping
cream

2 tablespoons
powdered sugar

½ ounce chocolate,
shaved

Shared recipes are more often favorites than originals. Someone sent Nanny a recipe that turned out to be very close to a classic Black Bottom Pie* from *The Joy of Cooking*. Its delicious crust is cleverly made from ginger snaps and it was just too good to leave out.

Layers and layers of sweet filling make a rich, rich pie in this old southern recipe. Start with chocolate custard spread on a gingersnap crust, add a layer of rum custard, and then top it off with whipped cream and shaved chocolate. After a fish fry, it's the pièce de résistance.

METHOD

Preheat the oven to 300°F.

Mix the gingersnaps with the melted butter and pat evenly into a deep 9″ pie pan. Bake for 10 minutes to set. Remove and let cool.

To make the custard, in a saucepan scald the milk. In a bowl beat the egg yolks with ½ cup sugar and the cornstarch. Add the hot milk gradually, stirring constantly. Heat in a heavy-bottomed saucepan or the top of a double boiler, stirring occasionally, until the custard thickens and generously coats a spoon. Remove from heat and take out 1 cup of the custard. To this cup, add the melted chocolate and beat well. When cool, stir in the vanilla and spread the chocolate custard in the cooled crust. Chill.

While the remaining custard is still hot, stir in the softened gelatin until dissolved. Set the pan in a pan of cold water and let cool, stirring occasionally, until the custard is almost ready to set. Meanwhile, beat the egg whites until frothy, add the

*Adapted with permission of The Bobbs-Merrill Company, a subsidiary of Macmillan, Inc., from *The Joy of Cooking* by Irma S. Rombauer and Marion Rombauer Becker. Copyright © 1931, 1936, 1941, 1942, 1943, 1946, 1951, 1952, 1953, 1962, 1964 by The Bobbs-Merrill Company.

cream of tartar, and beat until stiff. Then beat in the remaining ½ cup sugar gradually, and whip until the meringue is very stiff. When the custard is cool but still smooth, fold in the meringue and rum flavoring. Spread the fluffy rum custard evenly over the chocolate custard and chill for a few minutes until set.

Whip the cream until it holds a shape, sift in the powdered sugar, and continue beating until stiff. Spread the cream evenly over the rum custard. Sprinkle the shaved chocolate over the top. Chill until serving time.

NOTE: *Gold rum, such as Mount Gay, adds the best flavor to the vanilla custard.*

YIELD · 8 SERVINGS

CHESS PIE

The recipe for this classic Southern dessert came from Martha Houghton's mother, who was born in Tennessee in 1874. Unlike most meringues, the one mentioned here does not call for sugar and creates a fluffy foil for this rich, rich pie. It was quite a hit among family and friends and in 1928 was printed with her permission in a cookbook published by the Fort Worth Woman's Club.

METHOD

Preheat the oven to 375°F.

With an electric mixer beat the yolks for 1 minute. Then gradually add the sugar and beat for 5 minutes more, until light and fluffy.

In a separate bowl or a food processor cream the butter until light and fluffy. Add to the yolk mixture and whip together. Add the vanilla. Divide the mixture between the 2 piecrusts and bake for about 15 to 20 minutes, or until set.

While the pies are baking, whip the egg whites in a bowl until stiff. As soon as the pies are done, spread the meringue

INGREDIENTS

5 eggs, separated, room temperature

1 cup granulated sugar

¾ cup butter, room temperature

1 recipe Flaky Piecrust (page 212), chilled in 2 pie plates

1 teaspoon vanilla extract

over the tops and run under the broiler until lightly browned. Serve hot or warm.

YIELD · 12 SERVINGS

CHILLED PINEAPPLE PIE

INGREDIENTS

*½ recipe Flaky
   Piecrust (page
   212), chilled in 9"
   pie plate*

4 eggs, separated

*1 cup granulated
   sugar*

¼ teaspoon salt

*½ cup, plus 2–4
   tablespoons crushed
   canned pineapple*

*1 tablespoon lemon or
   pineapple juice*

½ cup pineapple juice

*4 tablespoons lemon
   Jell-O powder*

*¼ teaspoon cream of
   tartar*

If Nanny was partial to citrus-flavored desserts, Chilled Pineapple Pie could have been why. Essentially a cold soufflé or mousse, this recipe combined her penchant for meringue-topped pies with lemon and pineapple.

METHOD

Preheat the oven to 425°F., and bake the piecrust for 12–15 minutes. Remove from oven and cool.

In a double boiler or heavy-bottomed saucepan beat the egg yolks slightly and add ½ cup sugar, salt, ½ cup crushed pineapple, and the lemon or pineapple juice. Cook, stirring frequently, until the custard thickens and coats a spoon, 10 to 15 minutes. Heat the ½ cup pineapple juice and dissolve the lemon Jell-O in it. Stir this mixture into the custard. Set the pan of custard in a larger pan of ice water and let cool, stirring occasionally, until the mixture is on the verge of setting.

Meanwhile, in a bowl beat the egg whites with the cream of tartar until stiff, and gradually add the remaining ½ cup sugar to form a stiff meringue. When the custard mixture is cold but not yet set, fold in the meringue and pile into the cooled pie shell. Chill until set, then decorate the top with the remaining pineapple. Serve cold.

YIELD · 8 SERVINGS

LEMON MERINGUE PIE

 On any number of occasions, Martha Hough-ton's granddaughter Lisa reminded me to "be sure to include Nanny's Lemon Pie in her cook-book. You know how much we loved it." Here it is, light and tart, using Grandmother's recipe for Meringue Topping.

METHOD

Preheat the oven to 425°F. and bake the pie shell for 12–15 minutes. Remove and cool. Leave the oven on and lower to 400°.

In a heavy-bottomed saucepan sift 1 cup sugar, the cornstarch, and salt together. Stir to mix well and slowly add the water, stirring until smooth. Cook over medium heat, stirring occasionally, until boiling. Boil for 1 minute, stirring gently and often. The mixture will be very thick.

In a bowl beat the egg yolks lightly and whisk the hot cornstarch mixture into them. Then return the yolk mixture to the saucepan and cook for 1 minute, stirring. Remove the pan from heat and add the lemon juice and rind, mixing well. Let cool for a few minutes and pour into the cooled piecrust.

In another bowl beat the egg whites with the cream of tartar until the whites form stiff peaks. Then add the ¼ cup sugar, a tablespoon at a time, beating well after each addition. Spread the meringue evenly and decoratively over the lemon filling, sealing to the edge of the crust. Place the pie in the oven and bake for 5 to 7 minutes, until lightly browned. Remove and let cool.

Serve at room temperature.

INGREDIENTS

½ recipe Flaky Piecrust (page 212), chilled in 9" pie plate

1¼ cups granulated sugar

¼ cup cornstarch

⅛ teaspoon salt

1¼ cups water

3 eggs, separated

3 tablespoons lemon juice

Grated rind from 2 lemons

⅛ teaspoon cream of tartar

YIELD · 6–8 SERVINGS

PEACH (OR APRICOT) COBBLER

INGREDIENTS

6 cups fresh or
  defrosted peaches or
  fresh apricots,
  peeled and sliced

1/2 cup granulated
  sugar

1 tablespoon
  cornstarch

3/4 teaspoon ground
  cinnamon

2 tablespoons butter

1/4 recipe Lottie's
  Biscuits dough
  (page 71), uncut

1 cup heavy cream

If I were ordering what I knew had to be my last meal, I would probably ask for peach cobbler for dessert. Warm cobbler served with fresh heavy cream has always been a favorite at the Ranch. I can see it now, served in those Mexican hand-blown blue dishes brimming with hot peaches, flaky crust, and dripping with cream.

I can also recall one hilarious dinner when I was 13 and overweight. Nanny had just put me on a 2,000-calorie daily diet and given me a pamphlet on calorie counting. The dessert was cobbler and Nanny asked me if I wanted any. With typical adolescent lack of thought, I asked if it was fattening. Nanny howled, and so did everyone else. I had my answer, but if you want to know, I had a little cobbler, too.

Nanny had a great philosophy about keeping trim. She said it's not what you eat but how much. With her help, I shed a lot of pounds. Her moderate approach to enjoying food and "holding the line" has served me well.

METHOD

Preheat the oven to 425°F. Butter an 8″ square glass baking pan.

Place the peaches or apricots in a large bowl and sift the sugar, cornstarch, and cinnamon over them. Mix well and pour into the prepared baking pan. Dot with the butter. Place in the oven and cook for about 15 minutes, or until the peaches are hot and bubbly.

While the peaches are cooking, roll out the biscuit dough to an 8″ square. When the peaches are hot, remove the pan from the oven, quickly lay the biscuit dough over them, and return the pan to the oven. Bake for 15 to 20 minutes, until the topping is golden brown. Ladle or pour heavy cream on each individual serving.

YIELD · 6 SERVINGS

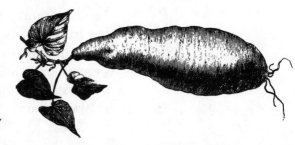

Sweet Potato Pie

If you like Southern sweet potato pie or Yankee pumpkin pie, this recipe should be quite pleasing. It's a bit drier than pumpkin, but just as spicy and more buttery. As for sweet potato, this version makes relatively light soul food.

METHOD

Preheat the oven to 400°F.

In a pot boil the sweet potatoes for 25 to 30 minutes, or until tender when pierced with a fork. Peel and mash or puree the potatoes.

In a bowl cream the butter and brown sugar well, then add the eggs and beat well. Add the salt, spices, pureed potatoes, and milk and mix well. Pour into the pie shell and bake for 45 minutes, or until a knife inserted in the middle comes out clean.

NOTE: *You can substitute 2 cups of canned sweet potatoes, mashed, for the fresh sweet potatoes.*

YIELD · ABOUT 12 SERVINGS

INGREDIENTS

1 1/2 pounds sweet potatoes (see Note)

1/2 cup butter

1/2 cup brown sugar

2 eggs

1/2 teaspoon salt

1/2 teaspoon ground ginger

1/2 teaspoon grated nutmeg

1 cup milk

1/2 recipe Flaky Piecrust (page 212), chilled in 10" pie plate

CUSTARDS AND

BAKED CUSTARD

This plain, basic recipe calls for 4 eggs and 1 quart milk. It never fails to draw raves from the little cowboys and cowgirls who crawl, walk, and then run around the Headquarters. Its appeal, though, is easily expanded to children of all ages with the clever addition of stewed apricots or jams such as strawberry or blackberry.

INGREDIENTS

4 eggs
½ cup granulated
   sugar
1 quart milk
1 teaspoon vanilla
   extract
Grated nutmeg
   (optional)

M E T H O D

Preheat the oven to 300°F.

In a bowl, beat the eggs, sugar, and milk together until well mixed. Add the vanilla and stir to blend. Pour into 8 ½-cup custard molds, set the molds in a pan of hot water, and bake for 1 to 1¼ hours, or until set. Chill.

Serve with a sprinkling of nutmeg, if desired.

YIELD · 8 SERVINGS

BOILED CUSTARD

This old standby is a staple at the Ranch. Nanny believed in its medicinal qualities and often served it to anyone whose appetite was off.

As a dessert ingredient, boiled custard makes a luxurious sauce. Try it for cake that tends to be dry, or on any poached fruit.

PUDDINGS

In a heavy-bottomed saucepan or in the top of a double boiler beat the egg yolks with the sugar. Gradually stir in the milk. Heat the mixture until it thickens enough to coat a spoon, about 180°F. Do not let it boil or the yolks will curdle.

Remove from heat, strain, and add the vanilla. Chill. Serve as a dessert, sauce, or cold beverage.

YIELD · 4 CUPS

INGREDIENTS

- *8 egg yolks*
- *6 tablespoons granulated sugar*
- *1 quart milk*
- *1–2 teaspoons vanilla extract*

APRICOT TAPIOCA CREAM

Some of the best surprises are often created when a time-honored recipe is changed just a little. Here, chopped apricots and strained apricots and applesauce are added to this old-fashioned favorite, giving it a tart edge that's really quite pleasing. Nanny's grandson Teddy Caldwell liked it so much that she used to save the warm mixing bowl for him to savor the last little bits.

M E T H O D

In a bowl beat the egg yolk slightly. Add the milk, tapioca, sugar, and salt and mix well. Heat in the top of a double boiler or a heavy-bottomed saucepan to boiling. Let simmer for 5 minutes. Remove from heat. Add the apricot-applesauce, lemon juice, and vanilla to the tapioca and blend well. Beat the egg white until stiff and fold into the mixture. Chill slightly, then fold in the diced apricots and chill thoroughly.

Serve plain or with whipped cream, if desired.

YIELD · 4–6 SERVINGS

INGREDIENTS

- *1 egg, separated*
- *2 cups milk*
- *3 tablespoons Minute tapioca*
- *1/3 cup granulated sugar*
- *1/8 teaspoon salt*
- *1 4 1/2-ounce jar strained apricots and applesauce*
- *1 tablespoon lemon juice*
- *1/2 teaspoon vanilla extract*
- *1 cup diced stewed or canned apricots, drained*
- *Whipped cream (optional)*

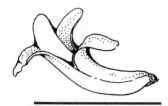

BANANA-MACAROON MOUSSE

This recipe was dated November 1927 and is another example of Nanny's fascination with using tropical fruits to add life to simple recipes. The mousse is surprisingly light for the heavy ingredients called for. You may want to try it with less sugar the first time around and then "season" it to taste.

INGREDIENTS

- 4 large bananas, or 6 small
- 1/8 teaspoon salt
- 1 1/2 tablespoons lemon juice
- 3/4–1 cup macaroon crumbs (4–5 macaroons, crumbled)
- 2 cups whipping cream
- 1/2 cup powdered sugar

METHOD

Puree the bananas in a food mill or food processor. Add the salt, lemon juice, and macaroon crumbs, and transfer to a bowl. In another bowl beat the cream until stiff, then add the sugar. Fold the cream into the banana mixture. Place the mousse in a 2-quart serving dish and freeze without stirring for 4 hours before serving.

YIELD · 8 CUPS · 8–10 SERVINGS

NATILLA

Nanny's version of this Tex-Mex dessert is a mousselike vanilla pudding flavored with brandy and rum. There's nothing quite like it after a dinner of her enchiladas and chiles rellenos.

INGREDIENTS

- 2 cups milk
- 3 eggs, separated
- 1/3 cup granulated sugar
- 1/4 cup all-purpose flour
- 2 teaspoons vanilla extract
- 1/2 tablespoon brandy
- 1/2 tablespoon amber rum
- Pinch salt
- Grated nutmeg (optional)

METHOD

In a saucepan scald the milk.

In another saucepan beat the egg yolks until thick. Add the sugar gradually, beating until thick and lemon-colored. Stir in the flour and beat well. Pour in the hot milk gradually, stirring constantly. Cook over medium heat, stirring, until the custard reaches a boil, and boil for 2 minutes, stirring. Remove the pan from heat, and let cool to lukewarm.

Stir in the vanilla, brandy, and rum. Beat the egg whites

with a pinch of salt until they form stiff peaks. Stir a quarter of the whites into the custard, then fold in the rest of the whites. Pour into 6 to 8 dessert dishes and chill until serving time. Sprinkle the tops with grated nutmeg, if desired.

YIELD · 6–8 SERVINGS

ORANGE PUDDING

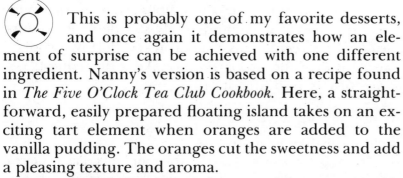 This is probably one of my favorite desserts, and once again it demonstrates how an element of surprise can be achieved with one different ingredient. Nanny's version is based on a recipe found in *The Five O'Clock Tea Club Cookbook*. Here, a straightforward, easily prepared floating island takes on an exciting tart element when oranges are added to the vanilla pudding. The oranges cut the sweetness and add a pleasing texture and aroma.

Due to the high moisture content of the oranges, this dessert does not store well, even if it is refrigerated. After more than 12 hours, the juice released from the orange sections makes the pudding appear to separate. The best thing to do is make it when there are four or more people to serve. There won't be any leftovers to store—or in this case, to argue over.

INGREDIENTS

3 eggs, separated

1 cup powdered sugar

1 1/2 tablespoons cornstarch

2 cups milk

2 teaspoons vanilla extract

3 or 4 oranges

1/3 cup granulated sugar

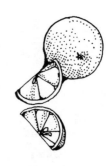

METHOD

In a heavy-bottomed saucepan or in the top of a double boiler mix the egg yolks, powdered sugar, and cornstarch. Stir in the milk gradually to make a smooth mixture. Add the vanilla and cook over medium heat, stirring constantly, until thick. Do not let boil. Remove and cool.

Preheat the oven to 400°F.

While the pudding is cooling, prepare the oranges: peel with a sharp knife and cut into either sections or slices, removing any pits. Lay the orange pieces in the bottom of an 8″ baking dish. When the custard has been thoroughly cooled, spread it over the oranges. Beat the egg whites until soft peaks form, then add the granulated sugar. Beat until stiff. Spread over the pudding. Brown in the oven for 3 to 5 minutes, on the top shelf.

YIELD · 4–6 SERVINGS

RICE PUDDING

This "double-egg" pudding turns an old family standby into an incredibly custardy rice pudding. It's easy to make and nicely studded with plump raisins. This recipe makes good use of leftover cooked rice. However, be prepared to make it on request. For lovers of rice pudding, it's that good!

INGREDIENTS

4 eggs, separated
2 cups milk
½ cup raisins
1¼ cups cooked rice
½ teaspoon salt
½ cup granulated sugar
⅛ teaspoon ground cinnamon or grated nutmeg
1 tablespoon powdered sugar

METHOD

Preheat the oven to 400°F.

Add 4 tablespoons milk to the yolks and mix. Place the rest of the milk in the top of a double boiler or in a heavy-bottomed saucepan and cook the raisins in the milk until they are soft and tender, about 15 minutes. Add the rice and cook for 5 minutes longer. Stir in the yolks mixed with milk, the salt, granulated sugar, and spice. Stir well, cook for 2 or 3 minutes, and pour into a serving dish.

Beat the egg whites until stiff, add the powdered sugar, and spread the meringue on top of the pudding. Place on an upper shelf in the oven for 2 to 4 minutes, until the top is delicately browned. Served cold.

YIELD · 6–8 SERVINGS

SWEET POTATO PUDDING

The common southern tuber takes on an elegant glow in this delightful dessert. In a custardy pudding with raisins, the sweet potato blends well with the nutmeg and butter and satisfies like Indian pudding or pumpkin pie.

M E T H O D

Preheat the oven to 350°F. Butter an 8″ baking dish.

Puree the sweet potato in a food mill or processor. Stir in all the remaining ingredients except the egg whites and cream, and mix thoroughly. Whip the whites until stiff and fold into the sweet potato mixture. Pour into the baking dish and bake for about 45 minutes, or until firm. Serve warm with cream.

YIELD · 4–6 SERVINGS

INGREDIENTS

- *1 large sweet potato (³/₄ pound), cooked and peeled*
- *¹/₂ cup raisins*
- *³/₄ cup granulated sugar*
- *2 eggs, separated*
- *2 tablespoons butter, melted*
- *¹/₄ teaspoon grated nutmeg*
- *1 cup milk*
  Heavy cream

PRUNE WHIP

As I polled family and friends for what recipes they'd like to have from the Houghton Ranch, I heard any number of times, "Be sure and get Nanny's recipe for Prune Whip." This version contains walnuts. It's fluffy as a soufflé, surprisingly light, and not cloyingly sweet. For an "old-fashioned" recipe, it is refreshingly appropriate for serving after a meal of wild fowl, roast pork, or veal.

M E T H O D

Preheat the oven to 350°F. Butter a 2-quart baking dish. Boil a pan of water for the baking dish to sit in.

Chop the prunes finely, or puree coarsely in a food processor. Stir in the sugar. Beat the egg whites until stiff and fold into the prunes, along with the nuts. Turn into the baking dish, place in the pan of boiling water, and bake for 35 to 45 minutes, until browned and firm. Serve hot or cold.

YIELD · 6 SERVINGS

INGREDIENTS

- *1 cup cooked pitted prunes*
- *4 tablespoons granulated sugar*
- *6 egg whites*
- *¹/₂ cup chopped walnuts (or pecans)*

FAR FROM THE RANCH

Martha Houghton passed on in October 1983 at the age of ninety. During her lifetime, she traveled far and wide, making many friends and collecting some interesting recipes along the way. They were obviously happy discoveries, and it's a pleasure to share them.

The recipe for Frosted Bread and Butter Pudding was probably found on a trip to England. Her version of Avocado Salad with Shrimp Sauce mostly likely derived from a dish she enjoyed in San Francisco. New York yielded Danielle's heavenly Cheese Soufflé and the cold beet soup called Borscht served in delicatessens.

Chicago, in spite of many visits, yielded nothing but laughs. Once known for its extensive stockyards, it was the locale for one of Unc's favorite dinner stories.

It seems there was a rancher who had a foreman who was born and raised on the place and had never ventured too far from home. Come the fall and roundup, the rancher decided he'd take his foreman to Chicago when he went to the famous stockyards to sell his cattle. When they got there, the rancher received word to come home for an emergency right away. Not to spoil the foreman's fun, the rancher arranged a line of credit for his cowboy and left him there to discover the big city.

Well, the foreman wasn't too comfortable with the hustle and bustle. He just stayed in his room except for going out to get his boots shined and buy cigarettes.

Finally, the cowboy and the cigarette girl struck up a conversation. She wanted to know how he liked the big city, and he explained how he really hadn't taken too much in. Of course, she offered to show him the town, and it wasn't too long before they ended up in his room.

After a few days together, he packed up and announced he was going back to the ranch. So, she followed him down to the train station where she asked, "How about some money?" "Aw, don't you worry 'bout that, ma'am," the cowboy drawled. "If yuh think of it, just send me a tie or something."

As for the remaining discoveries presented here, I'll just quote Nanny from one of her favorite recipes for beets: "Try these. Good."

TED HOUGHTON, RACONTEUR, ABOUT 1955

Avocado Salad with Shrimp Sauce

MOLD

6–7 ripe avocados
      (preferably
      California),
      halved

  4 tablespoons lemon
      juice

  4 envelopes of
      unflavored
      gelatin softened
      in ½ cup cold
      water

1¼ cups boiling
      water

  2 teaspoons salt

  1 teaspoon sugar

⅛ teaspoon cayenne

  1 small onion,
      pureed

¾ cup mayonnaise

SAUCE

½ garlic clove

  1 pint heavy sour
      cream

½ cup catsup

  2 tablespoons
      Worcestershire
      sauce

1½ tablespoons
      grated or pureed
      onion

  1 teaspoon salt

      (continued)

If only avocado trees could survive the sub-zero freezes of the High Plains, we might have enjoyed this wonderful salad at the Ranch more often. The light green avocado mold itself is cool and creamy, contrasting well with delicate shrimp in a piquant, pink sour cream dressing.

This dressing has great character and possibilities. It's equally good with crab or lobster and can double as a sharply flavored vegetable dip for crudités.

Scrape the pulp out of each avocado half. Press through a sieve or puree in a food processor. Add the lemon juice and blend well.

Into a bowl pour the softened gelatin, then add the boiling water and stir until dissolved. Place the bowl in a pan of cold water until it starts to congeal. Blend it with the avocado and add the salt, sugar, cayenne, and onion. Beat well and then beat in the mayonnaise, blending thoroughly. Pour into an 8-cup ring mold rinsed with cold water and spread evenly. Chill until firm.

To unmold the gelatin, gently separate the firm mixture from the edge of the mold with a long, thin knife in several places. Moisten the top surface of a well-chilled serving plate and quickly turn the mold over onto it. Slide the mold into the position desired. Next, steady the mold with one edge against the plate and gently shake, lifting the mold off. If this fails, drape the mold with a warm, damp cloth for just a few seconds and try again. (These tips can be found in *The Joy of Cooking*.)

For the sauce, rub a bowl with the garlic. Pour in the sour cream, catsup, and seasonings and blend well. Stir in the shrimp and serve.

To serve, ladle one cup sauce over the mold as if icing a Bundt cake. Serve the remaining sauce in a bowl to be passed and enjoyed at the table.

YIELD · 8–16 SERVINGS

2 tablespoons grated horseradish

¹⁄₄ teaspoon dry mustard

¹⁄₂ pound cleaned shrimp, cooked and chopped

JALAPEÑO SALSA JELLY

When it comes to happy discoveries, this lusty version of pepper jelly has to be one of the best. Made with ingredients for Gar's Chili Salsa, this jelly is lively and colorful. Served with cream cheese on a plain cracker, such as Carr's Table water biscuits, it's addictive. In fact, I've seen more than one guest make a meal of it!

METHOD

Chop the peppers, tomatoes, and onions in separate batches in a blender or food processor to produce ¹⁄₄″ to ¹⁄₈″ dice. Add the batches to a large saucepan as they are chopped.

Add the sugar and vinegar and bring to a full rolling boil and boil hard for 5 minutes. Pour in the pectin and boil hard for another minute. Skim any foam and preserve according to proper canning methods.

NOTE: *For a milder, less hot jelly, substitute pieces of green bell pepper for some of the jalapeños.*

YIELD · 6 ½ PINTS

INGREDIENTS

2¹⁄₂ ounces jalapeño peppers, washed, stems trimmed, and cut in halves (do not remove seeds and ribs)

¹⁄₂ pound plum tomatoes, washed, cored, and coarsely chopped

1 small onion, coarsely chopped

1 cup cider vinegar

6 ounces Certo liquid pectin

CHEESE SOUFFLÉ A LA DANIELLE

INGREDIENTS

4 tablespoons butter

½ cup all-purpose flour

1 teaspoon salt
Dash cayenne

2 cups milk

1 cup grated Parmesan cheese

6 eggs, separated

Martha Houghton found this recipe on one of her many trips to New York. Danielle's of Fifty-fifth Street, long gone, was famous for its soufflés. Its spirit lives on in the delicate toquelike soufflé produced by this easy recipe. Baked at the lower temperature, it rises surprisingly high and will literally melt in your mouth.

METHOD

Preheat the oven to 325°F or 425°F. Soufflés may be baked at 325° for 25 to 30 minutes, producing a delicate, moist soufflé throughout, or at 425° for 13 to 14 minutes, producing a darker, thicker crust with a moist inside.

Make a roux by melting the butter in a saucepan over low heat. Stir in flour, salt, and cayenne until well blended; the roux will be very stiff. Remove the pan from heat. Add the milk very gradually, stirring constantly. When smooth, return to heat, bring to a simmer, and simmer for 2 minutes. Add the cheese and stir until melted. Remove from heat and add the egg yolks, one at a time, stirring thoroughly after each addition.

Beat the egg whites until very stiff but not dry. Fold them carefully into the cheese mixture. Divide evenly among eight unbuttered 4″ soufflé dishes. Bake as directed above and serve immediately.

NOTE: *The soufflé mixture may be mixed in advance to the point where the yolks are added. Beat the whites and fold in just before baking.*

YIELD · 8 SERVINGS

CRAB LORENZO

This is another one of Martha Houghton's party dishes, which she probably collected on one of her hunting trips to the Gulf. I'd like to be able to claim that Nanny called it Lorenzo for me, but the date on her notes is 1947, and I wasn't born until 1949!

For entertaining, this recipe makes an elegant offering. The hollandaise browns beautifully over the crab and mushrooms in a satiny white sauce. For eye appeal, serve Crab Lorenzo on round-cut white toast.

M E T H O D

In a skillet heat the butter and sauté the onion and mushroom slices until soft. Add the chives, pepper, and crabmeat and blend well. Pour in 4 ounces Sauterne, cover the pan, and cook for 3 to 5 minutes. Remove the cover and cook until almost dry. Add the remaining ounce of Sauterne and stir in.

Using a 3″ biscuit cutter, cut rounds from the bread slices and then toast. Spoon the crab mixture onto the toasts, dividing evenly, and cover each with 2 tablespoons hollandaise. Run under a hot broiler to brown slightly and serve immediately.

YIELD · 8–10 SERVINGS

INGREDIENTS

- 2 tablespoons butter
- 1 medium onion, minced
- 6–8 large mushrooms, washed and sliced
- 1 teaspoon chopped fresh chives
- 1/2 teaspoon pepper
- 3/4–1 pound fresh, frozen, or canned crabmeat
- 5 ounces Sauterne
- 8–10 slices of white bread
- 1 1/2–2 cups hollandaise sauce, homemade or best quality prepared

INGREDIENTS

6 *tablespoons butter*

3 *celery stalks, washed and destringed with a vegetable peeler, finely chopped*

1/2 *green pepper, washed and finely chopped*

2 *6-ounce cans crab, or 3/4 pound fresh or frozen*

2 *tablespoons flour*

3/4 *cup clam juice*

1/4 *cup dry sherry*

3 *eggs, hard-cooked*

1 *teaspoon Worcestershire sauce*

1/4 *teaspoon pepper*

1/2 *teaspoon salt*

1 1/8 *teaspoons Old Bay Seasoning (see note)*

1–2 *tablespoons dry sherry (optional)*

16 *saltines, crushed*

DEVILED CRABS

No, crabs don't grow at the Ranch, and until recently, fresh seafood (let alone crabs!) was not available in the Panhandle. However, Martha Houghton frequently served this recipe made from canned crab and other fresh ingredients at parties to rave reviews.

METHOD

In a skillet heat 2 tablespoons butter and sauté the celery and green pepper until soft. Then add the crab and toss until mixed. Remove the mixture from the pan.

Melt another 2 tablespoons butter in the pan. Stir in the flour until smooth. Add the clam juice and sherry and heat, stirring, until the sauce is thickened and smooth. Return the crab mixture to the pan. Chop the eggs and add to the pan. Add the Worcestershire, pepper, salt, 1 teaspoon Old Bay Seasoning, and 1 or 2 tablespoons sherry and blend thoroughly. Taste and add more seasonings, if desired. Put the crab mixture in 6 to 8 shells or ramekins.

Mix the crushed saltines with the remaining 1/8 teaspoon Old Bay and sprinkle a generous tablespoonful of crumbs over each filled shell or ramekin. Dot with the remaining 2 tablespoons butter, cut into bits.

Place under a hot broiler until browned and heated through.

NOTE: *Old Bay Seasoning is available in specialty food shops. If you can't find it, poultry seasoning, such as Bell's, will do in a pinch.*

YIELD · 6–8 SERVINGS

RUBY WAGNER'S DEVILED EGG CASSEROLE

Ruby Wagner was a longtime friend of Martha Houghton and a regular member of their weekly lunch and penny ante poker games. No doubt, Mrs. Wagner made this recipe for one of their weekly luncheons and Nanny adopted it to become a popular item on her own menus. These eggs are especially good with Nanny's Cheddar Cheese Sauce, and they pick up a little extra eye appeal when sprinkled with toasted whole-wheat bread crumbs and bacon bits.

METHOD

Preheat the oven to 350°F. Butter a baking dish.

In a bowl, mash the egg yolks with the sour cream, mustard, salt, pepper, and ham. Adjust the seasonings to taste.

Stuff the egg whites with the yolk mixture and place in the baking dish. Pour the cheese sauce over and around the egg halves. Sprinkle with the crumbs, dot with butter, cut into small bits. Bake for about 30 minutes, or until bubbly.

YIELD · 6 SERVINGS

INGREDIENTS

- 12 eggs, hard-cooked and halved
- 6 tablespoons sour cream
- 1/2 teaspoon dry mustard
- 1/2 teaspoon salt
- 1/4 teaspoon pepper
- 4 ounces cooked ham, chopped
- 3 cups Cheddar Cheese Sauce (page 178)
- 1/2 cup bread or cracker crumbs
- 1 tablespoon butter

FROSTED BREAD AND BUTTER PUDDING

9 slices of firm
   bread, fresh or
   stale

3–4 tablespoons
   butter, room
   temperature

3/4 cup plus 1
   tablespoon
   currants

3 eggs, plus 2 egg
   whites

3 cups milk

1/3 cup plus 2
   tablespoons sugar

1 teaspoon vanilla
   extract

Nanny probably collected this recipe in England; the method directs the cook to "besprinkle" the pudding with black currants. Wherever she got the recipe, I am glad she saved it. A nice crusty, golden topping covers a rich vanilla custard with currants that—served warm—is ethereal.

M E T H O D

Preheat the oven to 325°F. Butter a 2-quart baking dish.

Trim the crusts from the bread slices and spread the slices with butter. Cut the slices into 1″ squares. You should have 4 cups of squares. Layer a third of the bread squares in the baking dish and sprinkle with ¼ cup currants. Repeat twice.

In a bowl, mix the whole eggs, milk, ⅓ cup sugar, and vanilla thoroughly; pour over the bread mixture. Let stand for 30 minutes, pressing the cubes down once or twice. Bake for about an hour, until lightly browned and not quite firm.

Beat the egg whites until stiff, beat in the 2 tablespoons sugar, and beat a little more. Remove the pudding from the oven and raise oven heat to 400°. Spread the meringue over the pudding, sprinkle with the tablespoon currants and brown in the oven for 3 to 5 minutes, on the top shelf. Serve at room temperature.

NOTE: *The meringue frosting can be omitted. The pudding is nice by itself.*

YIELD · 4–6 SERVINGS

SHRIMP BOIL

Martha Houghton probably acquired this on one of her many trips to Corpus Christi, where she and her husband Ted went to hunt and fish in the Gulf of Mexico. This method gives the shrimp a nice aroma of bay leaves and imparts a sharp, clean edge to their flavor. For an "edge" sharp enough to split hairs, split the chiles!

INGREDIENTS

- 2 quarts water
- 1 cup salt
- 4 hot pepper pods, halved vertically
- 4 bay leaves
- 1 lemon, halved
- 20 whole cloves
- 2 pounds large, raw shrimp

METHOD

In a pot combine all the ingredients except the shrimp and bring to a boil. Boil for 15 minutes. Add the shrimp and simmer 5–7 minutes or until pink. Drain at once and chill. Serve the shrimp in or out of the shell but devein before eating.

NOTE: *For a terrific seafood sauce, add grated or prepared horseradish to Nanny's "J.J." Barbecue Sauce according to taste. As a rule of thumb, one tablespoon of horseradish for every three tablespoons of barbecue sauce works quite well.*

YIELD · 2 QUARTS · 6 SERVINGS

BIBLIOGRAPHY

American Cooking: The Great West. Alexandria, Virginia: Time-Life Books, 1971.

Beutel, Jane. *Woman's Day Book of New Mexican Cookery.* New York: Pocket Books, 1984.

Cameron, Angus, and Jones, Judith. *L.L. Bean Game & Fish Cookbook.* New York: Random House, 1983.

Dawson, John. *High Plains Yesterdays.* Austin, Texas: Eakin Press, 1985.

Dent, Huntley. *The Feast of Santa Fe.* New York: Simon & Schuster, 1985.

Duke, Cordia. *Six Thousand Miles of Fence: XIT Ranch.* Canyon, Texas: Paramount Publishing, 1961.

Fast, Barry. *The Catfish Cookbook.* Charlotte, North Carolina: East Woods, 1982.

Five O'Clock Tea Club Cookbook, The. Fort Worth, Texas: The Five O'Clock Tea Club, copyright unknown.

Hibler, Jane. *Fair Game, A Hunter's Cookbook.* New York: Irena Chalmers Cookbooks, Inc., 1983.

Johnson, Elizabeth. *The Helen Corbitt Collection.* Boston: Houghton Mifflin, 1981.

Lilly, Clyde A. (Mrs.), and Davis, Olin (Mrs.). *The Woman's Club of Fort Worth Cookbook.* Fort Worth, Texas: The Woman's Club of Fort Worth, 1928.

Lone Star Legacy. Austin, Texas: Austin Junior Forum, 1981.

Out of the Skillet. Holly Springs, Mississippi: St. Anne's Guild of the Parish of Christ Church, 1947.

Robertson, Pauline D., and Robertson, Roy L. *Cowboy Country.* Canyon, Texas: Paramount Publishing, 1981.

Rombauer, Irma S., and Becker, Marion Rombauer. *Joy of Cooking.* New York: Bobbs-Merrill, a subsidiary of Macmillan, Inc., 1964.

Texas Experience, The. Richardson, Texas: The Richardson Woman's Club, 1982.

Trahey, Jane. *A Taste of Texas.* New York: Random House, 1949.

Udvardy, Miklos D. F. *Audubon Society Field Guide to North American Birds.* New York: Knopf, 1977.

RECIPE CREDITS

The author is grateful for the recipes/adaptations from the following sources:

Dawson, John. *High Plains Yesterdays*. Austin, Texas: Eakin Press, 1985.

Duke, Cordia. *Six Thousand Miles of Fence: XIT Ranch*. Canyon, Texas: Paramount Publishing, 1961.

Five O'Clock Tea Club Cookbook, The. Fort Worth, Texas: The Five O'Clock Tea Club, copyright unknown.

Lilly, Clyde A. (Mrs.), and Davis, Olin (Mrs.). *The Woman's Club of Fort Worth Cookbook*. Fort Worth, Texas: The Woman's Club of Fort Worth, 1928.

Robertson, Pauline D., and Robertson, Roy L. *Cowboy Country*. Canyon, Texas: Paramount Publishing, 1981.

Rombauer, Irma S., and Becker, Marion Rombauer. *Joy of Cooking*. New York: Bobbs-Merrill, a subsidiary of Macmillan, Inc., 1964.

Trahey, Jane. *A Taste of Texas*. New York: Random House, 1949.

Witty, Helen S. *The Flower Grower*. August 1964.

INDEX

Note: page numbers in *italics* refer to illustrations

ABOUT THE AUTHOR

Larry Ross, an avid cook, hunter, and fisherman, spent his boyhood at the Houghton Ranch and has returned there every summer since 1959. He lives in Stamford, Connecticut.